SUPPORT FOR MATTHEW COSSOLOTTO'S PROMISEPOWER IDEAS AND INITIATIVES AND THE POWER OF MAKING A PROMISE

"When Matthew first told me about the heartfelt promise he made to his mother and that he was launching a special day called "Make A Promise Day" on May 4th, I was hooked. You could say he had me at 'I promise' … There truly is something special about a promise, and I congratulate Matthew for shining a spotlight on this unique power through this book, his speeches and his workshops."

— Jack Canfield
From his Foreword to *Harness Your PromisePower*
Co-Creator of the *Chicken Soup for the Soul®* Series
Author of *The Success Principles.*
www.JackCanfield.com

"I have spoken with Matthew about his project related to the Power of Making a Promise … I agree completely … There is something uniquely powerful about making a promise that goes beyond traditional goal setting. I was delighted to share a personal story with Matthew about a very special promise I made in my own life. I believe Matthew's mission has the potential to be of enormous benefit to many others and I offer him my very best wishes for success in compiling these uplifting stories about

promises made and promises kept. Put simply, Matthew's project is very promising indeed!"

— John Assaraf
A leading high-performance coach,
entrepreneur and bestselling author.
www.JohnAssaraf.com

"You're onto something big here. Because when we make a promise, we put our word on the line, and we have to step up for it. I commend you on the work you're doing. It's an inspiration to me."

— Gail Lynne Goodwin
Founder, Inspire Me Today. www.InspireMeToday.com

"I made a promise to Madiba, and I intend to keep it."

— Oprah Winfrey
On her promise to Nelson Mandela

"If you have been looking for the 'key' to personal and professional success, here it is: Make important promises and keep them."

— Craig Womack and Jason Womack
The Promise Doctrine: A guidebook and system for consistently delivering on your promises!

"At that moment, I made a promise to myself! I promised at that rock bottom moment that I WAS NO LONGER GOING TO BE A VICTIM. I WAS GOING TO BECOME A VICTOR!... Once I made that promise to myself, I worked extremely hard, became even more disciplined, and stopped making excuses for myself. It took years, but I finally got my life back on track. Making that promise to myself was absolutely the best thing for me in my entire life!

— Marques Ogden
Former NFL player, keynote speaker,
and best-selling author. https://marquesogden.com

"A promise conveys: This is important enough to me that I'm going to promise to do it. I'm taking this very seriously, and I'm deeply committed to the outcome ... I look forward to supporting your "Make A Promise Day" in May and being part of this great campaign as it grows, and grows, and grows."

— Todd Newton
Emmy-winning TV host, author of
Life In The Bonus Round.
https://www.toddnewtononline.com

"Promises are the uniquely human way of ordering the future."

— Hannah Arendt

"Our Alliance was created by people who had lived through two devastating world wars... So, they founded NATO with a clear purpose: to preserve peace and to safeguard freedom. They made a solemn promise: One for all and all for one."

— NATO Secretary General Jens Stoltenberg
Address to a Joint Meeting of the U.S. Congress
April 3, 2019

"I know that I have the ability to achieve the object of my definite purpose in life; therefore, I demand of myself persistent, continuous action toward its attainment, and I here and now promise to render such action."

— Napoleon Hill
Think and Grow Rich

"This make-a-promise philosophy really resonates with me. The promise I made to my grandmother was always there and I knew she would be happy that I kept my promise to her."

— Stefania Lucchetti
Speaker, leadership expert, poet,
and author of *The Principle of Relevance*
www.stefanialucchetti.it/en/

"Leaders know that honesty and integrity are the foundations of leadership. Leaders keep their promises."

— **Brian Tracy**
Sales Training Expert and Bestselling Author

"I spoke with Matthew Cossolotto about the promise he made to his mother and his 'Power of Making a Promise' concept. I believe this truly is a Million Dollar Idea."

— **Norm Lapalme**
Entrepreneur, Coach, Founder of Ambassador Program.
www.ambassadorprogram.com

"Happy 'Make A Promise Day' everybody! I really like Matthew's idea. The power of making a promise to someone you care about really can change your life. Great work Matthew... May The Fourth Be With You!"

— **Rick Frishman**
Best Selling Author, Publisher and Speaker
www.RickFrishman.com

"It was in that dark hospital that I, for the first time in my life, made a promise to myself. In spite of everything Dr. Moberly had told me about my physical condition and the injury I had sustained, I promised myself that I was going to walk out of that hospital under my own power… Two weeks later, I walked out of the hospital on my own power."

— **Bill Bartmann**
Billionaire Secrets of Success

"I want to call your attention to an exciting and inspiring initiative created by my friend Matthew Cossolotto ... He calls it "Make A Promise Day" -- the first-ever "holiday" dedicated to personal empowerment and goal achievement. With "Make A Promise Day," Matthew is encouraging people to turn important goals into heartfelt promises. I really like that idea, and I thought it would appeal to you as well."

— **Brian Proctor**
Publisher of "Insight of the Day"
www.insightoftheday.com

"I was interested in knowing what causes someone who has struggled with being overweight to suddenly shift and find the strength to lose so much weight ... [JD Roth] said that people who choose to start at the simplest step, keeping a promise to themselves, even when no one is looking, begin to change how they behave. It is as simple as that. Those who succeed are those who decide they are worth keeping a promise to. Of course, this applies to all areas of life."

— **Lewis Howes**
Best-selling author and host of The School of Greatness podcast, describing his conversation with JD Roth, creator of the TV show "The Biggest Loser"
www.LewisHowes.com

"Being associated with Matthew's inspiring 'Make a Promise' project is totally aligned with my life's purpose."

From the Foreword by Jack Canfield,
Co-Creator of the *Chicken Soup for the Soul®* Book Series

CHANGE YOUR LIFE
TRANSFORM THE WORLD

MATTHEW COSSOLOTTO

Harness Your PromisePower

www.MatthewCossolotto.com

Book Cover Design and Interior Formatting by 100Covers.

First paperback and ebook editions February 2026

ISBN 978-1-7366976-1-0 (paperback)
ISBN 978-1-7366976-2-7 (ebook)

Published by
Flair Writers Group
170 Morgan Street
Oberlin, Ohio 44074
www.FlairWritersGroup.com

DEDICATION

To my big sister, Pattie. She always kept her promises.

CONTENTS

FOREWORD

A Promise Is a Promise: By Jack Canfield

A promise is a promise! I've heard that simple expression many times over the years. It's been etched indelibly in my mind since childhood. I'm not sure when I first heard somebody actually say those words, but I can't remember a time when I didn't believe them.

It's just one of those truisms. A fact of life. There are no ifs, ands or buts about promises.

A promise is a promise. Period. End of story.

That explains, in part at least, why I was immediately – you might even say instinctively – attracted to the central message of this important book. When Matthew first told me about the heartfelt promise he made to his mother and that he was launching a special day called "Make A Promise Day" on May 4th, I was hooked. You could say he had me at "I promise."

There was something very attractive, almost magnetic, about this concept. And I say that as somebody who has been intimately involved in the personal development field for many years. I've seen and heard just about everything.

Matthew and I first met at Steve and Bill Harrison's Quantum Leap Program in Philadelphia. If you haven't had the pleasure of meeting Matthew, let me tell you he can be very engaging and persuasive. He's not overbearing in any way, but he spoke that day with so much infectious passion and enthusiasm that I was eager to hear more. I gave him my personal email address and asked him to send me more information about his project. Matthew said he would, and I promised to take a look at the material.

That's right. I said those two magic words Matthew talks so much about: "I promise."

In preparing to write this foreword, I've been doing a lot of thinking about the power of a promise. And the more I think about it, the more it occurs to me that the act of making and keeping promises comes very close to being a universal value in human society.

Just consider what kind of world we would inhabit if people routinely made promises and broke them. Thank goodness – even with all the cynicism we see around us today – we still notice it when people break solemn promises. And we don't approve. There's still a stigma attached to breaking a promise, whether you're a political leader, a spouse or parent, a high-profile athlete or a celebrity. Promises matter. To a large degree, social cohesion depends on an underlying bedrock of trust. If you could no longer trust that other people were going to do what they say, society would fall apart. Chaos would reign.

My friend John Assaraf made an extremely important observation during his interview with Matthew for this book. "We are neurologically wired to keep our promises," John said. He's absolutely right. This is a keen insight that goes to the very heart of what this book and the broader "Make a Promise" message are all about.

There truly is something special about a promise, and I congratulate Matthew for shining a spotlight on this unique power through this book, his speeches and his workshops.

I have come to think of the power of making a promise as being somewhat akin to the moral in Russell Conwell's wonderful "Acres of Diamonds" lecture, which he delivered to over 5,000 different audiences between 1900 and 1925. Just as the farmer in Conwell's lecture unknowingly and tragically sold his diamond-rich farm and then set off on a futile quest for diamonds, many people ignore the powerful, life-transforming resources that we already possess and instead seek outside themselves for ways to change their lives, reach their goals and resolutions and make a positive difference in the world.

Perhaps after reading this book and learning more about the power of making a promise, more people will take advantage of this amazing, irresistible force for positive change – a resource that should be regarded as one of our greatest treasures in life. Metaphorically speaking, we all possess "acres of diamonds" within us, a new frontier in the form of the boundless power of making and keeping promises.

Webster's Dictionary informs us that the word "promise" comes from the Latin "promittere" – to send forth. A promise is defined as "a declaration that something will or will not be done, given, etc."

But this dry definition of "promise" fails to capture its truly inspirational meaning. In my experience, the very word "promise" evokes a strong feeling. And therein lies its unique power to transform. There's an extraordinary emotional connection to the word itself, a connection that is at once heart-centered, reassuring, resilient and extremely empowering. When Matthew refers to those two magic words – "I promise" – he taps into the mystery and the majesty of making a promise.

In their wonderful book, "Ask and It is Given," my friends Esther and Jerry Hicks conveyed the teachings of Abraham. Chapter Two bears this intriguing title: "We Are Keeping *Our Promise* to You – We Are Reminding You of Who You Are." And in that same chapter you'll find these remarkable words: "We write this book because we *promised* you we would. And now, as you hold this book in your hands, you are completing a *promise* you made as well." (My emphasis in italics)

I cite these promises in Esther and Jerry's book because the book you hold in your hands right now comes from the same feeling of heartwarming and joyful promise.

In his self-help classic, "Think and Grow Rich," Napoleon Hill underscored the importance of making a promise as a starting point in building the self-confidence needed to be successful in life. In a chapter entitled "Faith," Hill instructed readers to write down, memorize and repeat the following to themselves: "I know that I have the ability to achieve the object of my definite purpose in life; therefore, I demand of myself persistent, continuous action toward its attainment, and I here and now *promise* to render such action."

Hill also wrote about the importance of positive emotions: "It is essential for you to encourage the positive emotions as dominating forces of your mind and discourage – and eliminate negative emotions." He then added what he called a very significant statement of truth:

"Thoughts which are mixed with any of the feelings of emotions constitute a 'magnetic' force which attracts other similar or related thoughts."

In just a few sentences, Hill summarized what is frequently referred to as the "Law of Attraction," popularized for millions of people around the world by Rhonda Byrne in her movie and best-selling book, "The Secret."

With a promise, your heart and your emotions are fully engaged. Because of this, a promise is what I call a personal empowerment "two-fer," combining the Power of Intention with the Law of Attraction. And that is a very powerful combination indeed.

With a promise you state intention clearly and categorically, while your emotional connection to that promise sets the Law of Attraction in motion toward fulfilling that promise. A promise gets the ball rolling in a positive direction and keeps the ball rolling.

I believe there are three factors that are essential for success in life. I call these the "holy trinity" of personal achievement: Purpose, Passion and Promise. As I discuss in my book, "The Success Principles," I believe we're all born with a life purpose. Identifying, acknowledging and honoring this life purpose is perhaps the single most important thing successful people do in their lives. Successful people understand and pursue their life's purpose.

When you live your life "on purpose," everything seems to fall into place. You're doing what you love. As a result, the people, resources and opportunities you need for success seem to gravitate toward you. When you're on purpose, you also feel yourself being driven by boundless enthusiasm and unbridled passion. A life on purpose is, by definition, a life filled with passion. The two go hand-in-hand. A life that's "off purpose" is often filled with feelings of frustration and drudgery.

Henry David Thoreau observed that most people "lead lives of quiet desperation." In other words, most people lead lives that are not on purpose or filled with passion and enthusiasm. And that's a real tragedy.

I sum up my own my life's purpose this way: "To inspire and empower people to live their highest vision in a context of love and joy." Contributing the foreword to this book and being associated with Matthew's inspiring "Make a Promise" project are totally aligned with my life's purpose.

But what about that third "P" word I mentioned above – the word "promise" – and how does that link together with purpose and passion? Again, I see making a promise to do something as the commitment that gets the ball rolling with conviction and emotion and then keeps it rolling when one encounters obstacles and experiences setbacks. As Napoleon Hill suggests, it's essential for us to make a promise to pursue our life's purpose and cultivate a burning desire – a passion – to succeed.

Matthew makes the point that "a promise is like a goal on steroids." I heartily agree. As a firm believer in the power of goal setting, I applaud this refinement to the goal-setting imperative. Turning certain goals into promises – especially when publicly declared or made with conviction to an important person in your life – takes goal setting to the next level.

In "The Success Principles," I write about Principle #7 – "Unleash The Power of Goal Setting." In that chapter I recommend that you write down at least 101 goals you want to achieve in your life. I went through that exercise myself. and within 14 years I had achieved 58 of my 101 goals, including traveling to Africa, flying in a glider, learning to ski, attending the summer Olympic games and writing a children's book. Setting goals is critically important for achievement and success in life, however you define success.

While I shared many of my goals in that book, I didn't share a very personal and sacred promise I made to God one night in a dim apartment when I was 27 years old. Far beyond a goal, it was a promise of how I would live the rest of my life. It was, I realized many years later, a sacred oath to fulfill my soul's purpose, to fulfill my destiny.

A graduate student at the University of Massachusetts in Amherst at the time, I was in my apartment that night reading a book a professor had given me that he thought I would enjoy. The book was *Life After Life*, by Dr. Raymond Moody, describing his pioneering research into near-death experiences. A medical doctor, Moody had become fascinated with the cases of people who had clinically "died" but who, several minutes later, were revived and could subsequently remember what they had experienced while they were "dead."

Through interviews with many such people, Moody was able to discern a clear pattern to their experiences. First, after they had "died," they had the experience of leaving their bodies, floating upward and being about to look down upon their "dead" bodies.

They were then transported through a dark tunnel (often while hearing a high-pitched sound) toward a "being of light" that loved them unconditionally – a being that people tended to identify as Christ if they were Christian, as Buddha if they were Buddhist, or simply as a being of light if they were agnostic or atheist.

Then, in the presence of this loving being, these "dead" people reviewed their life with the purpose of seeing what lessons they could learn from it. Inevitably, they were informed by the being that they had to return to their bodies – which they did, though reluctantly.

What struck me most in reading the book that night was a single comment from one of Moody's interview subjects. He said that the being of light had asked him two questions before showing him a review of his life. The first was, "What wisdom have you gained from this life?" The second question was, "How have you expanded your capacity to love?"

Those two questions, more than anything else in the book, deeply impacted me. I came to the conclusion that the main purpose of our lives on Earth is to deepen our wisdom and to expand our capacity to love. I remember thinking – probably because I was studying education at the time – "Hey, there really is a final exam; there are two questions, and it's a take-home test!"

I also remember thinking, "Nobody is teaching for the test." There were no classes at any school or university on "Extracting Wisdom from Your Experience" or "Learning How to Love More Unconditionally." I had been mostly studying history, geography, mathematics and biology – all useful, but not critical to the love, joy and inner peace that had eluded me for so long. And while churches were exhorting us to be more loving, kind, compassionate and forgiving, nobody seemed to have an effective curriculum or methodology for teaching us how.

That night I made a promise to God that literally changed the course of my life: I promised I would spend the rest of my life learning and teaching others about wisdom and love.

I began by teaching workshops on self-esteem, relationships and the principles of success. Then I started gathering stories that I felt contained messages of love and wisdom that would inspire and enlighten others. These stories later formed the basis of the 1995 book, *Chicken Soup for the Soul*, which has grown into a series of more than 250 titles with more than 610 million copies in print in 43 languages.

That promise I made many years ago in my dim apartment in Amherst has led to a life more productive, impactful and fulfilling than I ever could have imagined when I was 27.

Not all our goals are of equal importance or equal urgency. What Matthew suggests is very much on-target: People should get into the habit of turning some of their goals into heartfelt promises. This is Matthew's ingenious "G.P.S. Success Formula" in action: From **G**oals to **P**romises = **S**uccess. Just like the GPS system in a car keeps us on track and moving in the right direction, the same is true of Matthew's G.P.S. Success Formula.

As you will read in the pages that follow, promises come in all shapes and sizes. Author and cancer survivor Roslyn Franken stepped on a scale and was shocked at how much weight she had gained. She immediately made a promise to herself to lose the extra pounds and live a healthier lifestyle – a promise has turned into a coaching and speaking business in which she helps others who want to follow a similar path.

John Assaraf – a spiritual entrepreneur and inspiring teacher with whom I had the honor of appearing in the movie "The Secret" – shared a moving account about the promise he made to God the day his sons were born. Decades later, John still gets choked up just thinking about that promise.

Oprah Winfrey made a promise to Nelson Mandela that she would build a school in South Africa. That heartfelt promise helped Oprah overcome obstacles and persevere despite numerous setbacks and complications.

Nancy Brinker promised her sister, Suzy, who was dying from breast cancer, that she would dedicate her life to building awareness and finding a cure for the disease. With that solemn promise – conveyed movingly in her book, "Promise Me" – Nancy founded the Susan G. Komen organization and launched a worldwide battle against breast cancer, bringing hope and comfort to millions.

Bill and Melinda Gates teamed up with Warren Buffett to create the Giving Pledge (www.givingpledge.org) inviting the world's richest people to join them in promising to give at least half of their vast wealth to philanthropic or charitable causes. More than 200 billionaires from 30 countries have signed up – among them Richard Branson, Ted Turner, Elon Musk, and Mark Zuckerberg – collectively promising that hundreds of billions of dollars will be donated to a wide variety of lifesaving and life-changing charities around the world.

Oral Lee Brown stepped into a first-grade classroom in East Oakland and made a promise to 23 students that she would pay for them to attend college if they stayed in school and graduated. She kept that promise and formed the Oral Lee Brown Foundation that has since helped hundreds more attend college.

These are just a few examples of heartfelt promises made and kept. And I would emphasize again the word "heartfelt." The single most important feature that distinguishes a promise from other kinds of stated intentions, goals, commitments, objectives or resolutions is the heart connection – the emotional and psychological element.

I applaud Matthew for collecting and celebrating these uplifting stories about promises made and promises kept. They are a needed antidote to much of what we see in the media about broken promises, all too often in the form of a scandal, misconduct or outright malfeasance. I understand it's important for us to know about misdeeds, especially on the part of public officials or when laws are broken along with promises. But one of the key principles of the Law of Attraction is that we get what we focus on. So, if we keep focusing on all the broken promises around us, we'll keep getting more and more of the same.

Ultimately, the process of change and achievement comes down to you … to your level of commitment, your ability to persevere despite your fears, doubts and setbacks, and your capacity to sustain that indispensable burning desire to succeed over time. Making a **Promise** to align yourself with your life **Purpose** and your **Passion** is an all-important first step in your journey. And as Matthew points out, paraphrasing the great Lao Tzu, a journey of a thousand miles begins with a single … promise.

I want to take a moment to congratulate you for picking up this book and reading this foreword. It says something meaningful about you. It says that you are willing to take charge of your destiny, and that you are receptive to new ideas to help you clarify your purpose, unleash your passion and reach your full potential and promise in life.

You have come to the right place because reading this book will help you do just that. So, I encourage you to take what Matthew calls "The Promise Challenge," turning your most important goals into heartfelt promises. Decide which goals you're willing to state in the form of a promise – to yourself, to God or to someone you care deeply about. In other words, which goals are important enough to you that you're willing to put your integrity on the line to achieve?

Because when all is said and done, we're left with that simple truth: A promise is a promise. So, choose your promises wisely … and make sure you keep them.

Jack Canfield, co-creator of the bestselling and beloved Chicken Soup for the Soul® book series and internationally recognized leader in personal development and peak performance.

"Promises are the uniquely human way of ordering the future."
– Hannah Arendt

INTRODUCTION

PromisePower: The New Frontier in Personal Change and Achievement

A Few Promise Stories to Kick Things Off – Oprah Winfrey, Brendon Burchard, LeBron James, NATO, Roger Federer, Bill Bartmann, President Joe Biden.
Introducing the Compound Word "*PromisePower*"
"Harness" and "Promise" Defined
What You'll Find in This Book: Instruction, Inspiration, Information

I hope you have already read Jack Canfield's generous and revealing foreword. If not, I encourage you to do so now – or at least soon. Jack very kindly lays out the rationale for this book about as well as any author could hope for.

I am deeply indebted to Jack for his active and vocal support for my *PromisePower* initiatives. In fact, I can't think of anyone I would rather have introducing and endorsing the ideas in my book – and to do so as lavishly and fulsomely – than Jack Canfield has done. He has been an inspiration to me personally for many years – and to millions of his devoted readers and fans all around the world.

This introduction will underscore several of the points Jack makes in his foreword. I will also do my best to build upon some of the groundwork Jack has laid so expertly.

A FEW PROMISE STORIES TO KICK THINGS OFF

For starters, I want to highlight the timing of this book's publication. 2025 marked the 25th anniversary of the promise I made to my mother. I told Jack the details of that promise when he and I first met, and Jack included a reference to my promise in his foreword. But Jack was not aware of exactly when I made the promise. It has occurred to me in recent years that publishing this book to commemorate the 25th anniversary of the promise would serve to underscore the importance I place on the power of that original promise. It truly is amazing to me to think that I made the promise 25 years ago.

To this day, I'm not exactly sure what prompted me to make the promise. The decision was spontaneous. It just felt like the right thing to do at that moment. I knew I was about to spend a few minutes alone with Mom, precious moments that we both knew would be the last time we would be together. And it just hit me that I wanted to give her something meaningful, something that would perhaps bring her a measure of happiness at that terrible time.

Here's the story in a nutshell. I made a promise to my mother on her deathbed that I would finish writing a book she had been encouraging me to write and dedicate it to her memory. Her face lit up and, fighting back tears, she said: "You *do* that, Matthew. You *do* that. This makes me very happy."

I'll tell you more about that promise – how it came about and what it meant to me – in Chapter One. For now, suffice it to say that I kept my promise. Emboldened by the power of that promise, I finished the book a few years later. And so, as I had promised, my first self-help book was published with the following dedication:

"In loving memory of my mother...

I did it, Mom! Finally. I can honestly say that this book would never have been completed had I not made that promise to you at home in Gasquet, California, a few weeks before you passed away. This vividly demonstrates ***the power of making a promise****, especially to your mother."*
[My emphasis.]

The book was titled *HabitForce! How to Kick the Habits of FAILURE and Adopt the Habits of SUCCESS.* [Author's Note: In the coming months, I plan to publish an updated edition as *Harness Your HabitForce*, making it the third book in my personal empowerment trilogy.]

A few years after publishing *HabitForce!*, I happened to re-read the dedication and found myself suddenly jolted by the phrase "the power of making a promise." It felt as if the words jumped off the page, grabbed me by the shoulders, and shouted out their full meaning: There truly is a unique power in making a promise... and this power is available to each one of us. We simply need to recognize that power and learn how to tap into it, how to harness it. And when we do, as I discovered in my own life, we can indeed change our lives in surprising ways and make a positive difference in the world.

On the heels of this epiphany, I realized that I had serendipitously stumbled upon an important mission: To share what I discovered about this amazing power of making a promise with as many people as possible.

I promptly made a promise to myself to do just that. I've done the best I could over the years, but I'm aware that I've only scratched the surface in fulfilling *that* promise – by speaking to various audiences, by posting videos and interviews on this topic, by writing articles and press announcements, by collecting and sharing inspiring promise stories along the way, and ultimately by publishing this book, complete with a remarkable foreword by Jack Canfield. Having Jack involved in this project has encouraged me to keep at it through lots of ups and downs, through various difficulties and distractions. To say this has been a long and winding road would be a serious understatement.

Jack's support has encouraged me to persevere and to think big. Hence the idea of launching of a national/international "Make a Promise Day" initiative. As I envision it, Make a Promise Day (often appearing as MAPD for short) is the only unofficial "holiday" dedicated to personal empowerment, goal achievement, and integrity enhancement. You'll read much more on MAPD later in the book, especially in Chapter 7.

I have also proposed creating some new traditions related to making and keeping promises – such as making promises on special days like Mother's Day or Father's Day or even on your own birthday. Why not give your Mother flowers or candy AND a meaningful promise on Mother's Day? Why not make a promise – instead of a wish – and blow out those birthday candles? Again, there will be a more detailed discussion about those ideas later in the book.

To prepare to write this book, I conducted extensive research about people whose promises powerfully transformed their lives and the lives of others. I've also experienced the great pleasure of having people spontaneously share their promise stories with me, be it during one of my workshops or standing next to me in line at the grocery store. You will find many inspiring promise stories sprinkled throughout this book, including accounts of promises made and kept by many well-known people. These stories have inspired me to imagine a series of books about *PromisePower* in relation to many people and situations, including a volume about promises that changed the world, promises that parents make to children (and vice versa), and one called *Celebrity Promises.*

On the celebrity front, Oprah Winfrey's promise to Nelson Mandela springs to mind …

WHAT'S YOUR PROMISE?

Oprah Winfrey's Promise to Nelson Mandela

On a visit to South Africa in 2000, Oprah Winfrey made a promise to Nelson Mandela that she would build an academy for underprivileged girls in South Africa. She pledged to donate $10 million for the project. When it was finally completed in 2007, the Oprah Winfrey Leadership Academy for Girls had cost Oprah $40 million. The campus consists of 28 buildings including computer and science laboratories, a wellness center, a library and a theater.

Despite cost overruns and other complications, Oprah was determined to keep her promise. In the middle of the project she explained to CNN why she didn't abandon the costly project: "I made a promise to Madiba (Mandela's nickname), and I intend to keep it."

That last sentence from Oprah echoes a refrain I've heard repeatedly. It sums up the unique power of making a promise. Put simply: *I made a promise ... and I intend to keep it*. To me, that pretty much says it all.

For his part, Nelson Mandela made a few promises at critical moments in his illustrious life. In 1990, following his release after spending 27 long years in prison, Mandela assured South Africans, "I will keep my ***promise*** to fight for a free and democratic society." [My emphasis.] His promise was dramatically fulfilled when he became South Africa's first post-apartheid president in 1994.

Mandela also promised to prioritize reconciliation and healing in a country deeply divided by apartheid. Beyond South Africa's borders, Mandela promised to support global peace and justice and to address urgent global challenges and promote ethical leadership.

You'll also read stories that emerged in a series of detailed "What's Your Promise?" interviews I conducted. After the publication of this book, I just may launch a podcast called "What's Your Promise?" to collect and celebrate more moving promise stories. More on that idea later.

I'm excited to share these uplifting promise stories and much more to empower you to harness your own *Promise-Power* – which I believe truly is a potent force for personal achievement and positive change in the world. I have come to believe that a promise made and kept creates a kind of positive karmic halo effect, an invisible force that brings about manifold beneficial outcomes, directly and indirectly. This invisible force is why I decided that Make a Promise Day must be on May 4th. The simple reason is that I wanted to be able to say: May the Fourth be with you, and I wanted that play on words to hint at the special force that comes from making and keeping a promise. You'll see more details about Make a Promise Day in Chapter 7.

In his foreword to this book, Jack Canfield shared the life-changing promise he made to God when he was 27 years old. Once again, I hope you have read Jack's foreword and that you're now aware of the promise he made to God as a young man.

Here's another powerful promise story that I've heard Jack describe several times. This story relates to the publication of the very first *Chicken Soup for the Soul* book. Difficult as it is to believe, the book had been rejected by 144 publishers. Finally, one small publisher said he would publish *Chicken Soup for the Soul* if he knew he could sell 20,000 copies. For several months, Canfield and his business partner, Mark Victor Hansen, collected written commitments from various people who said they "promise" to buy one or more copies of the book. One businessman promised to buy 1,000 copies. In the end, the publisher agreed to publish the book because Canfield had more than 20,000 promises to buy the book.

Those written promises sealed the deal with this publisher. And the rest, as they say, is history. Since then, more than **250** *Chicken Soup for the Soul* titles have been published. Approximately 200 **million** copies have been sold in the United States alone. The books have been translated into at least 43 languages, published in over 100 countries, and have sold more than **600 million** copies worldwide.

Talk about the power of a promise! Those initial 20,000 promises made a huge difference in the lives of millions of people around the world. And they were instrumental in helping Jack keep that heartfelt promise he made to God when he was 27 years old.

By discovering and harnessing your own *PromisePower*, you will become part of a very special community of people who have enlisted this power – this invisible force – to change their lives and the lives of others.

People like Brendon Burchard, a "New York Times" best-selling author, motivational speaker, and high-performance coach. After a terrible car accident at the age of 19, Brendon received what he calls "life's golden ticket" – a second chance. Today, Brendon is one of the most widely followed personal development trainers in the world and a bestselling author of several books, including *Life's Golden Ticket, The Millionaire Messenger*, and *The Motivation Manifesto*. Visit www.BrendonBurchard.com for more information.

And it all started with Brendon's heartfelt promise to God. As he described it:

"To this day I vividly recall the moment I physically pulled myself free from the twisted wreckage … The dashboard and doors had been crushed inward, trapping the driver and me …. We struggled for what felt like hours to escape that coffin-like confinement. I remember pulling myself through the windshield, standing on the crumpled hood of the car, looking down at my bloodied body, then up to the heavens. And that was the moment when everything changed.

"Since then, I've been striving to keep a promise I made the very moment I was handed my golden ticket …. I inwardly spoke these words, which I will never forget: 'Oh, God,' I thought, 'thank you, thank you for the second chance. I *promise* I'll earn it.'" [My emphasis.]

Since making that fateful promise, Brendon has dedicated his life to inspiring millions of people around the globe to share their voices with the world. I applaud Brendon for making and keeping that heartfelt promise.

Here's another potent story I came across. It's about people who manage to keep promises they make to themselves. Best-selling author and one of the top podcasters in the country, Lewis Howes (www.LewisHowes.com) describes his conversation with JD Roth, creator of the TV show, "The Biggest Loser."

Howes explains: "I was interested in knowing what causes someone who has struggled with being overweight to suddenly shift and find the strength to lose so much weight ...

"[Roth] said that people who choose to start at the simplest step, *keeping a promise to themselves*, even when no one is looking, begin to change how they behave. It is as simple as that. Those who succeed are those who decide they are worth keeping a promise to. Of course, this applies to all areas of life." [My emphasis.]

I want to underscore a key point here: *People succeed when they decide they are worth keeping a promise to.* This is a huge factor in determining whether a person will keep a promise. I've said it many times: When you make a promise, your integrity is on the line. Your sense of self-worth is also on the line. Are you worth keeping a promise that you make to yourself? Simply asking this question engages your emotions, and this is vitally important in determining whether you're likely to keep your word.

Here's another promise story to help set the stage for the chapters that follow. Like the promise stories already mentioned, this next story is a reminder that the power of a promise is not the exclusive province of personal development authors and self-help gurus. It's something we all can readily tap into.

An article about basketball legend LeBron James – published in the January 2025 issue of Cleveland Magazine – highlights the unparalleled power of a promise. The article states: "LeBron James wears a rubber band on his wrist ... the bracelet carries a bold statement: I Promise. The message reminds the superstar athlete of his mission — the one that's bigger than his goals on the court. His promise to uplift the community that made him."

So, LeBron James made a bold promise to himself, and he wears a rubber band on his wrist as a personal reminder and to proclaim his promise to the world.

Another powerful example is the solemn promise described by Jens Stoltenberg, the Secretary General of the North Atlantic Treaty Organization (NATO), on July 9, 2024, at the NATO 75th Anniversary Celebratory Event in Washington, DC:

"Seventy-five years ago, in this very room, NATO's founding document, the Washington Treaty, was signed. Our Alliance was created by people who had lived through two devastating world wars. They knew only too well the horror, the suffering, and the terrible human cost of war. They were determined that this should never happen again. So, they founded NATO. With a clear purpose: To preserve peace and safeguard freedom. A solemn *promise*. An ironclad commitment to protect each other. One for all, and all for one." [My emphasis.]

A key point to underscore about this mutual defense promise among NATO members is this: A promise like this changes the behavior and expectations of others. The countries who join NATO understand that fellow members will come to their defense if their country is ever attacked. Promises have consequences because others trust that you will keep your word. We'll encounter this phenomenon repeatedly in the following pages. People take promises seriously. Which means you should take your promises seriously too.

Some promise stories presented themselves to me in unexpected places, including in movies and novels and even stories in the media.

For example: On Friday September 9, 2022, in his inaugural address as King following the death of Queen Elizabeth II, King Charles III said: "Queen Elizabeth's was a life well lived; a promise with destiny kept and she is mourned most deeply in her passing. That *promise* of lifelong service I renew to you all today." [My emphasis.]

Another example: Here's a heart-warming promise story from the world of professional tennis. In 2017, 36-year-old Roger Federer – one of the greatest tennis players of all time with 20 Grand Slam titles – made a promise to a six-year-old aspiring tennis player named Izyan ("Zizou") Ahmad. Zizou had an opportunity to speak with Federer at a tennis event. He asked this question: "Mr. Federer, can you please continue to play for eight, nine years so that I can play you when I go pro?" Federer replied, "Yes." "Is that a promise?" Zizou asked. To which Federer responded: "Pinky promise."

Five years later, the 41-year-old Federer was still playing tennis and Zizou, 11 years old at that time, was ranked as the No. 1 player under age 12 in the U.S. in both singles and doubles. Zizou came to Switzerland (Federer's home country) for a training event. Little did Zizou know that Federer had orchestrated this event so he could keep his promise to the young tennis star. Federer and Zizou played tennis together that day, and Zizou could not have been happier.

Afterwards, Federer posted the following on his official Instagram account: "One of the great benefits of this unbelievable sport are moments like these. Zizou, all the best and keep working hard. P.S. I always keep my pinky promises."

Very sweet! It's obvious that Federer put his heart into his promise to Zizou. Here's the key point. Making a promise is different from setting a goal, because a promise melds together thought or intention with feeling, emotion. That's why I often say a promise is like a goal on steroids. A promise comes from the heart, but a goal is more cerebral. When you add the heart connection by turning your important goals into heartfelt promises – voila! That's when the magic begins.

I very much appreciate what Jack Canfield wrote about the difference between making a promise and setting a goal in his foreword. "Matthew makes the point that 'a promise is like a goal on steroids.' I heartily agree. As a firm believer in the power of goal setting, I applaud this refinement to the goal-setting imperative. Turning certain goals into promises – especially when publicly declared or made with conviction to an important person in your life – takes goal setting to the next level."

Jack amplifies his point later in his foreword: "Not all our goals are of equal importance or equal urgency. What Matthew suggests is very much on-target: People should get into the habit of turning some of their goals into heartfelt promises. This is Matthew's ingenious "G.P.S. Success Formula" in action: From **G**oals to **P**romises = **S**uccess. Just like the GPS system in a car keeps us on track and moving in the right direction, the same is true of Matthew's G.P.S. Success Formula."

In his bestselling book *Billionaire Secrets of Success*, Bill Bartmann also makes a point of differentiating promises from goals. He recommends that we don't label something we want to accomplish a "goal." He says we should call it a "promise."

Why? Because he believes, and I agree wholeheartedly, that "promises are more powerful than goals." Bartmann discovered this difference because of the promise he made to himself at the age of 17 when he was paralyzed from the waist down and told by doctors that he would never walk again. I hope you'll read that inspiring story in Chapter 4.

Here's another example of the power of a promise in action. I noticed a promise at the very end of a long, engrossing article in the March 31, 2025, issue of "The New Yorker" magazine ("Open Secrets: Why did police let one of America's most prolific predators get away for so long"). The writer, Ronan Farrow, introduces readers to a wide array of people involved in a complicated crime story involving a local businessman in Johnson City, Tennessee. In November 2020, a federal prosecutor named Kat Dahl was assigned to the case.

The sordid details of the case do not concern me for the purposes of this book. Suffice it to say that Kat Dahl was eventually fired from her job as a prosecutor, but she continued to pursue the case as a private citizen. "All I want is some accountability in this case," Dahl wrote after being fired. Farrow's article concludes with the following quote from Kat Dahl: "I'm not done, and this story's not done. Way back in 2021, I told some of the victims that I was going to try and find them answers and find them accountability for what happened. ***I still intend to keep that promise.***" [My emphasis.]

Readers can track down the article in "The New Yorker" if they're so inclined. But I don't mention this article because of the details of the convoluted case. I cite the article because of the powerful word at the very end: ***Promise***. That word obviously meant a great deal to Kat Dahl. She knew the promise she made to some of the victims held a special kind of meaning to those victims and a special power that compelled Kat to pursue the case despite the hardships that she encountered along the way. This underscores the fundamental point of this book, a point I repeat several times in these pages: There is something uniquely powerful about making a promise.

I happened upon this next promise story while watching some videos about former Beatle, Sir Paul McCartney. McCartney was being interviewed on a 2023 Australian television program called 7.30 – hosted by Sarah Ferguson. Sarah asked McCartney why he had decided to return to Australia for an upcoming concert tour – his fourth tour Down Under. His answer sums up the power of a promise. He said: "Well… I said I would. So, I'm keeping my *promise*." [My emphasis.]

He said the words casually, but the message was clear: Keeping a promise is important. It almost goes without saying.

In his book, *Promise Me, Dad*, former U.S. President Joe Biden recounts the moving story about his son, Beau, who was losing his battle against brain cancer. Close to the end of his life, Beau asked his father to promise him that he would be OK after Beau passed away.

At first, Biden responded vaguely that he would be OK. But that wasn't good enough for Beau. He made his father promise, PROMISE, that he would be OK, that he would not use Beau's death as a reason to turn in but as a reason to turn out, to continue to be engaged and not to withdraw from public life.

Joe Biden made a heartfelt promise to his dying son. Hence the title of the book: *Promise Me, Dad*. It's my personal belief that Joe Biden decided to run for President of the

United States at least in part because he made that promise to his son.

This story captures the unique potency of the word "promise" itself. As mentioned, I have come to believe that a promise made and kept creates a kind of positive karmic halo effect. Good things happen when you keep a promise.

"HARNESS" AND "PROMISE" DEFINED

With these examples of real-world promises in mind, I think it would be helpful here to consider how I'm using the words "harness" and "promise." I want to make sure we're on the same page about the fundamental meaning of these two words.

First, I'm using the verb "harness" in the following sense, as defined in most dictionaries. To harness something is to… **control it, usually to make use of its power.**

The dictionary offers this sentence: "There is a great deal of interest in harnessing wind and waves as new sources of power." The same sense applies to harnessing solar energy. The goal is to tap into this source of power. To make use of it. For the sake of clarity, here are a few more synonyms that capture how I'm using the word "harness" in this book: to use, to utilize, to exploit, to apply, to employ, to exercise, to draw upon, to make use of, to channel, to mobilize, to make productive, to render useful. I think you get the idea.

Regarding the word "promise," with slight variations dictionaries define "promise" this way:

As a noun, the word "promise" refers to "a declaration or assurance that one will do a particular thing or that a particular thing will happen." The verb "promise" means to "assure someone that one will definitely do something or that something will happen."

When we look up "promise" in a thesaurus, we're presented with these synonyms – words that have a similar meaning: Vow, assurance, pledge, guarantee, warranty, pact, obligation, covenant, commitment, oath, and bond. I believe the word "promise" stands alone among these kindred words with the degree to which a promise comes from the heart backed by strong emotion.

Note also that the words "goal," "intention," "declaration," and "resolution" are not considered to be synonyms of the word "promise." "And thereby hangs a tale," as Shakespeare might say. In fact, this very book hangs on the difference between a promise and these other ways of stating a commitment. As Jack discussed in his foreword to this book, a promise brings much more emotion to the table than these other goal-oriented words.

These other tools for stating our goals or making commitments are much more cerebral. They simply don't pack the same emotional punch as a promise. They lack the same heart-centered potency.

INTRODUCING THE COMPOUND WORD "*PROMISEPOWER*"

Readers will note that I am introducing the compound word "*PromisePower*" and that it always appears in italics in the text. The point is to suggest there is something unique going on here. My intention is to introduce and to "own" the term "*PromisePower*." It is a special kind of power. It relates to personal empowerment. *PromisePower* has to do with turning important goals into heartfelt promises. And I often refer to these kinds of promises as "personal empowerment promises." *PromisePower* is a particular brand of power. I also introduce in this book and in my speaking programs a special wristband called a *PromisePower* Band. More on that to come.

WHAT YOU'LL FIND IN THIS BOOK - INSTRUCTION, INSPIRATION, INFORMATION

This book itself is intended as an antidote to the toxicity of cynicism and hypocrisy so prevalent in the world today. This book, moreover, is a tool to help you thrive in your own life and to improve the lives of those around you. As you read these pages, you'll see that this book – and my "Make a Promise" mission generally – embrace and extol an old-fashioned virtue: Each of us must take responsibility for our own life. This means, at a minimum, we must do what we promise to do.

The transformative power of this book comes from combining Three I's: Instruction, Inspiration, and Information. You'll learn potent new ideas and how to implement them. You'll be inspired by the real-life stories of people who have at least one thing in common: They made a solemn promise, and they followed through. And in so doing, they changed their lives and the lives of others. And you'll glean information about the power of promises based on research and other sources of data and insights.

INSTRUCTION: PRACTICAL STEPS TO A PROMISING FUTURE

The instructional, self-help components of this book provide insights, guidance, practical tips, and suggestions about turning your important goals into heartfelt promises and successfully following through. I refer to this as the G.P.S. Success Formula™ –

From Goals to Promises = Success

Like a navigational GPS system, the G.P.S. Success Formula keeps you on track. It keeps you moving in the right direction. I encourage you to take the "Promise Challenge." In Chapter 4: Make a Promise, you'll learn about supercharging your goals by turning them into promises that you "put your heart into." In Chapter 4, I also describe the three main types of promises and detail exactly how to make an effective promise.

In Chapter 5: Keep Your Word, I offer an assortment of time-tested tips and tools packed with transformational punch for keeping your promises, from "The Six Axioms of Personal Empowerment" and an easy-to-use rubber band technique for helping you keep promises and "snap out of" disempowering habits.

In Chapter 6: Change Your Life, you'll learn about psyching yourself up and staying on track with tools like positive self-talk and personal empowerment exercises. And you'll find my "Promise-A-Day Program: 30 Days to a Promising Future." The notion that people can use the power of making a promise as a personal empowerment tool isn't widely appreciated or employed. But it is embraced by a global organization called Optimist International. This association of more than 2,900 Optimist Clubs around the world is dedicated to "Bringing Out the Best in Kids."

Optimist International is well known for "The Optimist Creed" by Christian D. Larson. A version of this classic of positive thinking first appeared in Larson's 1912 book *Your Forces and How to Use Them*. It was not dubbed "The Optimist Creed" at that time. Instead, it appeared in the first chapter of Larson's book under the heading "Promise Yourself." Optimist International adopted "Promise Yourself" as The Optimist Creed in 1922.

The Optimist Creed boils down to a collection of what I call "Personal Empowerment Promises" (PEPs). A slightly abridged version of Larson's inspiring words appears today on Optimist International's website. [Visit https://www.optimist.org/member/creed.cfm.]

These and many more instructional components provide practical, how-to guidance and key steppingstones on your way into this exciting new frontier in personal change and achievement.

In Chapter 7: Transform the World, you'll be invited to join me in creating a worldwide "Make A Promise" movement. You'll learn about "Make A Promise Day" on May 4th, an annual, unofficial "holiday" dedicated to personal empowerment, goal achievement, and integrity enhancement. Make A Promise Day (sometimes appearing as MAPD) speaks to a key message of this book: That the solution to our problems, and the problems of the wider world, isn't "out there" somewhere, but is "in here," inside each one of us. Each of us can harness our *PromisePower* to change our lives and transform the world in wondrous ways.

Finally, you'll find details in the Appendix about where to send your personal promise stories (or inspiring promise stories you come across) for possible inclusion in future editions of promise-related books in this series.

INSPIRATION: REAL PROMISES BY REAL PEOPLE

As you have already seen, the inspirational element of this book consists of real stories from and about real people, including Jack Canfield, Oprah Winfrey, Brendon Burchard, former President Bill Clinton, Anthony Robbins, Danny and

Marlo Thomas, John Assaraf, Nancy Brinker, Al Roker and many others. I underscore here that many of the promise stories in the book are from everyday people, unheralded individuals who were willing to share their personal stories of promises made and kept. I view those stories to be especially powerful and inspirational.

I discovered that most people are excited about sharing the details of an important, even life-changing, promise they made to themselves, to someone they care about, or to a higher power. I discuss the importance of these three categories of promises – the three "who-to's" – in Chapter 5: Anatomy of a Promise.

As the phenomenal success of the *Chicken Soup for the Soul* series taught us, real stories about real people have the power to move and inspire others. By compiling and sharing inspirational stories about real people and the promises they made and kept, this book provides entertaining and unforgettable case studies of *PromisePower* in action.

These snapshots into the lives, struggles, and triumphs of others offer you accessible stories about the importance of making and keeping promises, even in tough times and often against incredible odds.

To date, these stories of personal change and achievement – stories of overcoming enormous odds and making a difference through the power of making a promise – simply have not been compiled and made easily available to readers around the world. Accounts of a promise made and kept are often tucked away in individual biographies or memoirs of famous people. Or they've been scattered widely in various media profiles and one-off human-interest feature stories. This book compiles many of these stories into one volume, thereby shining a much-needed spotlight on these moving personal accounts of promises made and kept. I hope you will enjoy them and be inspired by them. As mentioned, I also hope you will send me details of a life-enhancing promise story from your own experience.

Alternatively, I invite you to send me details of promises you come across in your daily life – promises made by friends or relatives or stories you read or hear about in movies or novels. Uplifting promise stories are all around us. I encourage readers to be on the alert for more of these powerful stories and help me share them with the world.

In future books in this series, I plan to share many more such stories – inspirational stories about Celebrity Promises, for example. And success stories from readers – maybe even you. So, as you read this book, I hope you will think about any life-changing promises you've made and consider sharing your story with me for possible inclusion in future volumes in this series. Instructions for doing so can be found in the Appendix. There might be books in the future that focus on specific categories of promises – such as promises made by parents to their children or promises made by teachers to their students. Perhaps there are many inspiring stories waiting to be collected about young people who made heartfelt promises to their grandparents or parents or people who made promises to improve the lives of others living in their communities. The potential topics and categories of promise stories are virtually unlimited. Please use your imaginations and feel free to suggest possible topics for future books on the power of promises.

INFORMATION: RESEARCH, DATA, QUOTES AND INSIGHTS

Throughout the book, you'll learn about research studies and their findings, compelling quotes and other insights about the power of promises in human history, among children and in society generally. This component offers you a wealth of useful ideas and information to bolster your confidence in the proposition that there is unique power to be found in making and keeping promises. This power has been remarked upon over the centuries and it has been confirmed by recent studies. But it has been oddly under-reported and under-appreciated in the human potential and self-help arenas.

Chapter 3 describes the sources of our *PromisePower*, starting in childhood and continuing throughout our lives. These sources include our parents and other adult role models, as well as books, movies, stories, spiritual teachings and other methods for transferring values and beliefs from one generation to the next.

On a few occasions, you'll be invited to gain greater self-awareness and personal insights through what I call "Inward Bound" exercises. I highly encourage that you do these rewarding exercises and that you keep a *PromisePower* Journal to record your ideas, your experiences, your insights, your goals, and most of all your promises and any promise-related stories you experience personally or come across.

HARNESS YOUR *PROMISEPOWER*: YOUR SECRET WEAPON

Harnessing the power of making a promise isn't complicated. And it's not even a "secret weapon" because just about everybody knows about it already. Still, I've often wondered why this remarkable power to transform lives goes largely unmentioned by self-help authors and personal empowerment coaches. This power seems like something of a new, untapped frontier in personal achievement.

Or more accurately, perhaps, it has been a largely overlooked frontier, the undiscovered country. Hidden in plain sight. Promises, in fact, are all around us. As Jack put it in his foreword, "Promises are part of the cultural zeitgeist, the foundation of ideals and beliefs that our society operates by." But like the proverbial fish that doesn't notice the water it's swimming in, we don't notice the power of a promise at our very fingertips.

In the following chapters, I hope to open your eyes and your heart to the uniquely human and uniquely potent power of making a promise, a make-or-break power that has the potential to change your life and, beyond that, to transform the world. Thank you for joining me on this journey of adventure and self-discovery. The next stop on that journey is to appreciate something we all know from childhood. There's something magic about those two powerful words: "I promise."

"When Matthew first told me about the heartfelt promise he made to his mother and that he was launching a special day called "Make A Promise Day" on May 4th, I was hooked." – Jack Canfield

CHAPTER 1

I Made a Promise to My Mother on Her Deathbed

My Make-a-Promise Mission
The two magic words: "I promise."
Take The Promise Challenge
Put Your Heart Into It
Introducing the Four-Part Mantra

As promised in the introduction, here is a more detailed account of the promise I made to my mother 25 years ago.

Here I am with my mother at a Parisian café a few months before her cancer diagnosis.

This photo evokes cherished memories of a visit to Paris that I made with my mother – her first and, tragically, her only visit to the City of Light. Just a few months after this photo was taken, Mom was diagnosed with lung cancer that had already spread. Within a year after this trip, she passed away … but not before I made the fateful promise mentioned in the Introduction. This was my gift to her and, it turned out, also her gift to me.

Virginia – or Ginny, as friends and family affectionately called her – had always dreamed of seeing Paris, a long-deferred dream during the years she spent raising my sister, brother and me pretty much on her own in the San Francisco Bay Area. Working full-time in a series of secretarial jobs, coming home at the end of a long day to make dinner and help with homework and tuck us into bed, Mom somehow managed to make ends meet, which frequently entailed packing us all up to move to a cheaper place. Taking a trip to Paris was certainly not in the cards for my mother back when we were kids. But many years later, I was fortunate enough to have the financial resources to make my mother's dream vacation in Paris come true.

This photo shows us at Les Deux Magots, the famous Paris café on Boulevard Saint-Germain. We had walked for hours that day through the city's beautiful streets and were quite exhausted by the time we sat down for coffee and a few late afternoon pastries. Not that you'd know it from our smiling faces in this photo. We were having a great time together. To this day, I'm amazed at how much energy Mom had during that trip. She was in her late 70s and still "full of vim and vigor," as she would have put it.

My mother and I had always enjoyed each other's company. Even after I left California for job opportunities in

Washington, DC, and then New York, we stayed in close touch via long-distance phone calls and occasional letters. We covered a lot of ground in our conversations, from family news to Shakespeare to politics.

We also spent many hours by phone and in person kicking around lots of different ideas, including some half-baked ideas that Mom thought I should turn into a book. At one point in the late 1990s, I explained to my mother that I had read Stephen Covey's bestseller *The 7 Habits of Highly Effective People.* And I found myself wondering, if there are seven habits of highly effective people, the must also be seven habits of highly *ineffective* people. She got a kick out of that. She said it was a clever idea to focus on the opposite of Covey's seven effective habits. I began to think of these seven habits as habits that hold people back from achieving their goals and dreams. I talked to my mother about this, and she completely "got it," which made it great to brainstorm with her about it.

One day it struck me that habits that hold people back could be called "failure" habits and suddenly I realized that the world "failure" has seven letters. That was my first epiphany. But, "failure" habits would be the opposite of "success" habits, not ineffective habits. And that's when it hit me: The word "success" also has seven letters. The creative light bulbs were flashing. I wondered aloud to my mother whether I might be able to create two side-by-side, seven-letter acronyms (actually "acrostics," but I've decided not to fight that losing battle). I envisioned each letter in the word "FAILURE" standing for a failure habit and each letter in "SUCCESS" representing a corresponding habit of success. An equal but opposite habit.

Wow! I thought. *How strange that these two powerful words in the English language, these two polar opposites – FAILURE and SUCCESS – should both contain seven letters!*

I began talking with a few friends and colleagues about some of these ideas. I recall specifically suggesting to others that I just might be the first person in history to notice that these two *yin-yang* words in our culture – failure and success – both have seven letters, and that perhaps two side-by-side acronyms could be created to help people recognize and remember these habits of SUCCESS and FAILURE. One word was empowering, the other disempowering.

The pieces of the puzzle were beginning to come together … in theory. But I doubted that I would be able to come up with an acronym for the seven habits of FAILURE and another acronym for seven habits of SUCCESS. The idea of doing so was intriguing but challenging.

I was convinced that these two, side-by-side acronyms could serve as a handy mnemonic device that would help people make the shift from failure habits to habits of success. That was the basic idea.

I shared these concepts with my mother during our frequent brainstorming conversations. She loved it so much that she said I should write a book about it!

Aren't mothers great? This was a wonderful thing about Mom: She had great faith in my abilities. By then I'd moved on from working in the Speaker's Office on Capitol Hill to a career as a speechwriter and corporate communications executive, and I had written a couple of books about European politics, so I knew a thing or two about writing. But the thought of writing a self-help book about the habits of SUCCESS and FAILURE was distinctly outside my comfort zone.

SOMETHING MAGIC ABOUT THE NUMBER "SEVEN"

Urged on by my mother, I continued to mull over the potential of writing a book based on these two seven-letter acronyms. I had to admit, there was something exciting about this idea. For starters, there's something magic about the number seven which added to the intrigue. There are numerous Biblical associations with sevens, beginning with The Book of Genesis. There's a sense of completion, some say perfection, in the number seven, with God resting on the seventh day. The Book of Revelation is replete with references to sevens.

And let's not forget the Seven Deadly Sins. Here's a refresher: Pride, Envy, Gluttony, Lust, Anger, Greed, and Sloth. For the sake of balance, we shouldn't ignore the Seven Heavenly Virtues either: Faith, Hope, Charity, Fortitude, Justice, Temperance, and Prudence.

It's also worth noting here that Mahatma Gandhi created his own "Seven Deadly Sins," which he humorously also called the Seven Blunders of the World: Wealth without work, Pleasure without conscience, Science without humanity, Knowledge without character, Politics without principle, Commerce without morality, and Worship without sacrifice.

More generally ... just think of how prevalent the number seven is in many cultures and in our everyday lives. In numerology, seven is the most spiritual of all numbers. Then there's the lucky number seven in dice ... the seven seas ... seven dwarfs (for the record: Sneezy, Sleepy, Dopey, Doc, Happy, Bashful, and Grumpy) ... seven days of the week ... seven Lucky Gods in Japan ... seven Wonders of the World ... seven fundamental musical notes ... seven plagues ... seventh heaven ... seven ages of man (in Shakespeare's "As You Like It") ... seven major Chakras ... seven pillars of wisdom … Seven Samurai … seven colors in the rainbow (in case you're wondering: red, orange, yellow, green, blue, indigo, and violet) … Also, Deepak Chopra's *Seven Spiritual Laws of Success* and the centerpiece of my own book, *The Joy of Public Speaking*: A chapter called "The Seven Steps to Joy." Last but not least, the book that started it all – Stephen Covey's *The 7 Habits of Highly Effective People.*

Finally, in a book about the power of a promise I would be remiss if I failed to mention that the word "promise" itself contains seven letters. And this book intentionally has seven chapters.

FAILURE TO LAUNCH COMEDY TV

In the interest of full disclosure, I should come clean about something. As I pondered these ideas about the seven habits of success and their failure counterparts, my ruminations weren't altogether a mere intellectual exercise. Nor was I wondering only about *other* people's habits. I was thinking, at least in part, about my own habits and mindsets. Some that helped me succeed in achieving my goals, and others that weren't quite as helpful – to put it mildly.

One episode, in fact, was still haunting me at the time, nearly 10 years after it occurred. That situation concerned my failure to launch Comedy TV. I describe this unfortunate episode in much more detail in my book *HabitForce!* and in the forthcoming edition *Harness Your HabitForce.*

I'll spare you most of the excruciating, if revealing, details in this retelling. I can sum up what happened in a few words: I blew it cuz I didn't pursue it. Sure, I felt badly about dropping the ball on what I thought was a great idea, but I pushed those feelings of regret away. I told myself it didn't really matter, that it probably wasn't going to work anyway.

That disheartening experience prompted me to embark upon a personal quest to learn more about what separates people who succeed from those who fail or just muddle through. The difference between those who start and lead successful businesses and those who just talk about doing so. That quest led me to Covey's book and those long conversations with my mother about habits of success and their opposite habits of failure.

As infectious as my mother's confidence in me could be, I hadn't really come around to her way of thinking. I didn't really think of myself as a self-help author. Besides, I wasn't sure I had what it would take to write such a book. Despite spending a fair amount of time thinking about the book, I was taking my sweet time actually writing the book. There's a big difference between talking a good game and actually getting into the game.

I procrastinated and made excuses: I had a busy life: a family, a full-time job and numerous other obligations. Months passed, and my mother kept asking me about the book. A year passed. And then another. Then, out of the blue, Mom was diagnosed with lung cancer. That was my wake-up call.

I visited her in California as often as I could, and we kept in touch by phone, but communicating became increasingly difficult as the cancer took its toll. On one visit home it was painfully clear that Mom was fading fast. She knew – my whole family knew – that this would be my last visit. The hospice nurse said she could go at any time and that she was ready.

That's when I made my promise.

It just came to me – a sudden flash of intuition, a "this is the right thing to do" inspiration. Sitting beside the bed in her dimly lit room, I searched for the right words. That whispered conversation will be forever etched upon my memory.

Holding her hand gently, I said, "Mom, you remember that book idea we've been talking about, the one about the habits of failure and success?"

Her eyelids were heavy from the morphine, but she was alert. "Yes," she nodded.

"Well," I said, "I decided to make you a promise. I promise to finish writing the book ... and dedicate it to your memory." Choking up with emotion, I could barely get the words out. I had uttered those two magic words: I Promise.

I watched her face intently, to make sure my words had registered. There was a long silence – I remember hearing the rushing sounds of the nearby Smith River – and then I noticed Mom was blinking back tears.

I'll never forget the look on my mother's face. Her eyes lit up and she smiled brightly, despite the terrible pain she was in. And somehow, fighting through fatigue and weariness, she raised her hand and jabbed an index finger in my direction.

"You do that, Matthew!" she said, her face an expression of steely determination.

"You do that!" she repeated and then whispered: "This makes me very happy."

We both fought back tears. Both acutely aware that she would not live long enough to see the book published or read my dedication to her.

When it came time to leave, I leaned over her and gave her a kiss on her forehead and a long goodbye hug. I knew this was our last goodbye, yet I left uplifted knowing that the promise I made had brought her some measure of happiness.

In the years since, I always think of that promise as the best gift I could have given to my mother before she passed away.

But also, through those passing years, I discovered that this gift to my mother also became her gift to me, because making that promise transformed my life. And I knew my mother would always be there, by my side, supporting me in fulfilling that promise and following the paths and opportunities that emerged as a result. Every time I conduct a workshop or give a presentation, I think about the promise I made and how it changed the trajectory of my life.

In making this heartfelt promise to my mother under the most painful of circumstances, something inside of me shifted: I knew that failure was not an option. I was going to write the book come hell or high water. I had crossed the proverbial Rubicon. There was no turning back, no making excuses. And what had been a vague "someday" goal of writing my book miraculously morphed into an inspiring mission, propelled by the power of making a promise.

One powerful lesson I took away from the promise I made to my mother is that you might not always know exactly where a promise will take you. It can lead you serendipitously in the right direction and open many unexpected doors and connect you with the right people along the way. I refer to this as the "positive karmic halo effect" of making and keeping a promise.

My promise gave me the enduring motivation to keep working on *HabitForce!* even though I wasn't sure if I could write the book or what I was going to do with the book once it was done or what, if anything, might come next.

And with this new book about harnessing your *Promise-Power*, I think about the profound discovery that began with my heartfelt promise to my mother. I appreciate the discovery of unexpected heart-centered power and determination that I felt propelling me toward keeping my word. And this discovery has become my compelling mission. Here's how I describe it:

My "Make-A-Promise" Mission

I promise to share the power of promises with millions of people around the world, to help them turn important goals into heartfelt promises. Together we can transform the world, one person and one promise at a time.

Whenever I think about this audacious mission – see Chapter 7: Transform the World for more details – I can almost hear my mother's voice encouraging me to publish this book and pursue this mission with enthusiasm and determination: "You do that, Matthew," she encourages me. "You do that. This makes me very happy."

THE TWO MAGIC WORDS: "I PROMISE."

Remember when you were a kid and you thought of "abracadabra" or "open sesame" as magical words that opened doors and unlocked storehouses of treasure? Words like these, you later learned, were fairytale figments of the imagination. But I'm here to tell you that two genuinely magical and powerfully effective words really do exist. These two magic words are "*I promise.*"

Little did I know twenty-five years ago – when I told my mother "I promise" – that ultimately this would become my mother's gift to me, setting me on a fresh path in life and leading me to discover – and ultimately share via this book and related articles, interviews, and presentations – the incredible power of those two simple and magical words.

If you're serious about achieving a specific goal – I mean *really* serious – you should state the goal in very clear, precise words to someone you care about and then say the two magic words: *I promise.*

"Words are events, they do things, change things," noted the renowned writer Ursula Le Guin. "They transform both speaker and hearer; they feed energy back and forth and amplify it."

This is especially true of the words "I promise." These two words are dramatically transformative. When you say, "I promise," you generate an unstoppable force that propels you in the direction of your goals and dreams, aligns the stars and virtually ensures your success. That's why I encourage the use of these two words in the service of what I call "personal empowerment promises." That is, promises that move you toward an important goal, toward reaching your peak potential.

This is why I think of harnessing your *PromisePower* as the new frontier in personal change and achievement. A promise helps you go from inertia to action. It's a palpable force that makes people sit up and pay attention – yourself included. When you say, "I promise," people sense that something about you has changed. You are inspired, illuminated by a fire inside of you that burns with emotional energy and heart-centered enthusiasm.

And the best news of all is that this inner fire is ignited not by something you must go out and hunt for. Instead, it's fueled by a power you already possess – that we all possess – in inexhaustible abundance, whether you happen to be aware of this or not. This book is dedicated to helping you tap into and harness your innate power of making a promise.

PROMISES ARE HEARTFELT

The unique power of the words "I promise" stems from the fact that a promise is heart-centric – heartfelt, coming from the heart and backed by deep emotional commitment. And with your emotions involved, you have some real skin in the game. Making a promise to someone you care about connects you to that person in a very special way. You become accountable on a deep, emotional level, and your personal integrity is on the line. Failure is not an option.

Setting goals, stating intentions, making declarations or resolutions are all very useful tools for setting your future course and clarifying what you would like to achieve. But goals tend to be more cerebral, more brain-centric in nature – not exclusively, of course, but predominantly – than making a heartfelt promise. Even the way we talk about goals differs from how we talk about promises. You can *change* a goal, but you can only *break* a promise. And most people are loath to break their promises. As John Assaraf says: "We are neurologically wired, I believe, to keep our promises ... There is something uniquely powerful about making a promise that goes beyond traditional goal setting. Setting a promise takes it to a whole new dimension."

This book focuses on the manifold positive benefits of making and keeping promises. I often refer to a kind of positive karmic halo effect of keeping promises. But I feel I should at least mention what happens when promises are broken. This gives rise to a dark karmic cloud because a broken promise can generate hurt feelings, disappointment, even trauma. A person who breaks a promise is often plagued by a sense of guilt or remorse.

Mahatma Gandhi once said: “Never make a promise in haste.” Gandhi also admonished: “A breach of promise is a base surrender of truth,” a sentiment that captures Gandhi’s belief in the importance of integrity and honesty. He understood that keeping a promise was key to building trust and meaningful relationships.

So, the message throughout this book is clear: Don’t break promises. Only make a promise if you plan to keep your word. Be aware that your integrity is on the line.

Here’s an inspiring story about a woman who made a bold promise. She knew from the start that failure to keep her word was not an option. Oral Lee Brown’s daring promise made a positive difference in her life and the lives of many others...

WHAT’S YOUR PROMISE?

Oral Lee Brown’s Promise to Send 23 First-Grade Students to College

[https://www.oralleebrownfoundation.org]

As a substitute teacher in Oakland, California some 30 years ago, Oral Lee Brown made an audacious promise to an entire classroom of first-grade students at Brookfield Elementary School.

“I walked into a classroom in one of East Oakland’s toughest neighborhoods, took a look at 23 first graders who nobody thought would amount to anything, and made them all a promise: ‘If you stay in school and graduate, I’ll send you all to college.’” In her book, *The Promise*, which she wrote nearly two decades later, Oral Lee recounted the extraordinary story.

Brookfield Elementary was, and still is, in a school district where the chances were slim that students even graduated from high school, let alone went on to college. But Oral Lee, convinced that her promise would make a difference in the lives of those first-grade students, now took steps to see her promise fulfilled. On the financial front, she knew that she'd need a lot more than the $45,000 a year she was earning at the time as a part-time teacher and realtor, so she saved and invested thousands of dollars year-after-year and built a substantial college fund. On a more personal level, she also "adopted" the students, developing close personal relationships with each one of them.

And when 19 of the 23 original first-graders students graduated from high school and enrolled in college, Oral Lee was there for them, paying their way and cheering them on.

In 2003, LaTosha Hunter became the first of the students to graduate from a four-year college. She was the first person in her family to accomplish this. When a local newspaper interviewed LaTosha on the day she received her bachelor's degree in accounting from Alcorn University in Lorman, Mississippi, she credited Oral Lee Brown.

"Everyone has a purpose in life, and her purpose was that we had a better life," said LaTosha, who went on to pursue a master's degree at Jackson State University.

Oral Lee has since established the Oral Lee Brown Foundation, which has further multiplied the magic of her promise. So far, the foundation has paid the way for 150 students who otherwise could not afford to attend college.

Oral Lee's moving story clearly captures the unique power of making a promise, a power that is yours to draw upon the instant you make a promise.

Stated simply, a promise can be more powerful than a goal because it comes from the heart and is charged with emotion.

Another powerful example involves a promise that led to the 2018 release on NetFlix of Orson Welles's last movie, "The Other Side of the Wind." Welles worked on the movie sporadically in the 1970s and early 1980s. The film was plagued by delays and complications, often stemming from lack of funding. At one point, Welles said to actor and executive producer Peter Bogdanovich: "If anything ever happens to me, I want you to promise me you'll finish the picture." Bogdanovich demurred saying that nothing is going to happen to Welles. But Welles insisted and Bogdanovich promised.

As fate would have it, Welles died before the movie was completed. Eventually, after a protracted legal and financial struggle to finish the picture, Bogdanovich kept his promise to Welles. NetFlix's advertising states that Orson Welles's last movie was "40 years in the making." In fact, it took 40 years for Bogdanovich to finally keep his promise to Orson Welles. And it's fair to conclude that the film would not have been finished if it weren't for that promise Welles elicited from Bogdanovich. As Bogdanovich explains in a documentary about the film: "I just felt I owed Orson to make good on the promise." That sums up quite succinctly just how powerful a promise can be. It continued to motivate Peter Bogdanovich 40 years after he made the promise to Orson Welles.

Sometimes a promise to do something is the result of a dare or a challenge put to you by someone else. There's no shame is responding to a challenge with a heartfelt promise.

Such was the case with actress and author Nancy Irwin. Nancy told me the story of how she happened to make a promise to become a stand-up comedian. Turns out she was prodded into the promise by a theatre critic in her native Atlanta, Georgia. I won't mention any names in this retelling of her promise. It seems this critic gave her rave reviews for her acting prowess, but he also encouraged her to try her hand (and her mouth, I assume) at stand-up comedy. He thought she was a natural comedian.

A few years passed, and Nancy had not yet taken the plunge into stand up. The theatre critic paid her a visit in New York City where she was acting, writing, singing, and modeling. She confessed to him that she had not yet tried stand up. Disappointed, he walked over to a wall-mounted chalkboard in Nancy's kitchen and wrote the following message: "If you do not try stand up by the next time I'm here, then you have no balls!"

That challenge was all it took. As Nancy tells the story: "I promised him I would. And I kept those words glaring at me, daring at me, for years! Actually, they stayed on that chalkboard for six years when I left NYC to move to Los Angeles, as a professional stand-up comic."

Nancy kept that promise, born of a dare. She also shared an impressive epilogue. After ten years as a comic, Nancy changed careers again at the age of 44. She is now a Los Angeles-based therapist. And she couldn't be happier. This shift in careers makes perfect sense for the author of a best-selling book titled, *You-Turn: Changing Direction in Midlife.*

TAKE THE "PROMISE CHALLENGE" … AND WATCH WHAT HAPPENS

As these examples demonstrate, the promise-driven life is readily available to each of us. And it begins by taking what I call the Promise Challenge, which is simply this: Go ahead and make a promise. Think about something that you'd like to achieve in your life. Whether it's a big ambition or just a small step, make a promise to do it … and then watch what happens.

The potential benefits are unlimited. Everything you need to power up your dreams is in the power of a promise. A power, let me remind you, that you already possess.

No matter what your life looks like right now or how it feels, you are fully equipped to take it to a whole new level. Maybe you tell everybody your life is just fine, but deep down you long to be doing so much better. So much more. No problem. You *can* do better. You can be all you think and believe you should be.

Or maybe you'd admit that things really aren't so great, that you feel burdened with frustration and a sense of falling short of your potential. You needn't worry. That weight can be lifted from your shoulders, and you can reach for the proverbial sky. An abundant universe brimming with potential for whatever you desire is completely within your reach. And the fact that you've picked up this book and are reading these words testifies to your readiness to embrace that abundance and reach your peak potential.

Do you want to be happier? Find more love and give more love? Be healthy, strong and fit? Have all the money you want? Even have great wealth? Would you like to have work that you find meaningful and fulfilling?

Or how would you like find and create opportunities to contribute your unique goodness to the world, just like Oral Lee Brown and so many others?

"The promise-powered life can be yours."

Like most people, I've grappled with frustration and failure, celebrated achievement and success – and experienced pretty much everything in-between. Along the way, I've been fortunate to experience the catalyzing power of a promise to make life-changing leaps from inertia to action. My discovery of the energizing and liberating power of a promise guides my life and serves as my inspiration in writing this book.

I can't wait to share with you everything I've learned about this amazing, make-or-break power.

THE THREE "MORES" YOU REAP FROM MAKING A PROMISE

Take the Promise Challenge, thereby harnessing the power of making a promise, and you will reap three main rewards that build one onto the next. You will:

Achieve More: By regularly turning important goals into heartfelt promises, you will dependably achieve your goals in a more effective and powerful way.

Believe More: As you achieve more, you will believe more in yourself and in your ability to reach your goals more consistently. This enhanced level of self-belief will enable you to continue to achieve even more in your life.

Receive More: As a result of achieving more and believing more, you will also receive more. This is important. I'm not saying that receiving is the be-all and end-all. But I think that too many of us have trouble receiving the things we want in our lives, from material possessions to loving relationships to spiritual growth. But when you're actively engaged in the process of achieving more and believing more, you will naturally become more comfortable exercising the power and the art of receiving.

One important point: To receive more, you must be grateful for what you already have. An attitude of gratitude will help you unlock the full power of a promise, and the full power to receive more in your life.

INTRODUCING THE FOUR-PART MANTRA

Your *PromisePower* holds the key to your success in making positive changes in your personal and professional life. In the process, you also make a positive impact in the world around you. I sum it up with the following four-part mantra:

Make a Promise
Keep Your Word
Change Your Life
Transform the World

Does transforming the world sound like too ambitious a goal for your promises? Well, it's not. Again and again, the world has been made a better place, one person and one promise at a time. A world of promise and possibility is the result of the accumulation of individual promises realized. So don't sell your promises short. Recognize that your promises – large and small, made and kept – have the power to transform the world.

Kody Bateman (https://www.sendoutcards.com) made a promise after the death of his brother. Bateman writes: "I ignored a prompting to say goodbye to my brother, Chris, when moving across the country. Two months later, I received the tragic news that my brother had been killed. I promised from that day forward to act on my promptings and help others do the same."

That emotion-charged promise led to the creation of SendOutCards, a business dedicated to helping people act on their promptings by sending cards and gifts to family members and friends.

Jack Canfield, in his foreword to this book, described the bold, life-changing promise he made to God when he was 27 years old. "I promised I would spend the rest of my life learning and teaching others about wisdom and love," a mission he fulfills to this day.

"Many people ignore the powerful, life-transforming resources that we already possess and instead seek outside themselves for ways to change their lives, reach their goals and resolutions and make a positive difference in the world," Jack noted in his foreword. "Perhaps after reading this book and learning more about the power of making a promise, more people will take advantage of this amazing, irresistible force for positive change – a resource that should be regarded as one of our greatest treasures in life."

Precisely!

The power of a promise is available to you – to all of us – right now. It's a power that comes naturally to you, me, everyone. Think about it: We all grasp immediately, on a gut level, what it means to make a promise. The very word "promise" resonates with us and has a special kind of meaning. That's not so surprising, really, given that we've been instructed since childhood about the sanctity of making and keeping promises. We feel good about ourselves when we keep promises, and we feel badly for letting ourselves or someone else down when we fail to keep our promises.

The power of a promise was underscored twice in a presentation by author and motivational speaker Jim Rohn. In the first instance, Rohn described a promise he made to himself when he was 25 years old. He was married, a father, hardworking but he was barely getting by financially. One day a Girl Scout knocked on his door. She described the various cookies she had for sale for $2.00. Rohn was too embarrassed to tell the Girl Scout that he didn't have $2.00 available to buy a box of cookies. So, he fabricated a humiliating lie. He told her that his family buys lots of Girl Scout cookies and they still have many boxes in the pantry. The Girl Scout thanked him for buying their cookies and left. But Jim Rohn was devastated about his financial situation. He made a promise to himself then and there to change his life, to explore ways to improve his finances, to find a path toward greater prosperity. Fortified by that powerful promise, he embarked on a life-transforming mission of self-improvement and personal empowerment.

Rohn also tells a story about giving a talk to some school children about how to be successful. In his presentation he discussed the importance of having resolve and he asked the children if they could define the word "resolve." One girl raised her hand and said that resolve meant making a promise to do something. There's that magic word "promise" again. Rohn said that was the best definition of "resolve" he had ever heard. In effect, making a promise operationalizes your intention. It turns a resolution into action backed by heartfelt commitment.

WHAT'S YOUR PROMISE?

Jamal Galves Makes a Promise to Save Endangered Manatees

Jamal Galves, a native of Belize, has been passionate about protecting wildlife since childhood. From the age of 12, he knew he wanted to work with animals – specifically manatees.

He has served as an associate research scientist with the Clearwater Marine Aquarium, Clearwater, Florida. Based in Belize, Jamal has been passionate about saving endangered manatees.

Jamal spent years working to protect the manatees and he has been recognized for his dedication. He was awarded the prestigious Ocean Hero Award by Oceana Belize for his passionate and heroic work with the endangered manatee. He has received the Belize National Hero Award (Meritorious Award) from the Belize Government for his conservation contribution to the country. He has also been named a National Geographic Explorer and a NatGeo PhotoArk Edge Fellow.

To say Jamal has been passionate about keeping his promise to the manatees would be a gross understatement. Here's how Jamal describes his promise in his own words:

"While I rescue these animals to safety, it gives me purpose. It makes me realize that what I'm doing is more than just awareness. It's literally giving a species another chance to live in the wild where it should be. And one of the promises I've always made to the Manatee was: 'Wherever I am and whatever I am doing, if you're ever in need I'll be there.' That's a promise I hope to keep for the rest of my life."

A PROMISE IS LIKE A GOAL ON STEROIDS!

As the above examples should make abundantly clear, making a promise is much more powerful than any other approach to setting goals in life. Put simply: A promise is like a goal on steroids!

Why? Because promises are heart centered. The very word "promise" is much more powerful than antiseptic-sounding, cerebral words like "goal," "objective," "decision," "declaration" or "resolution." A promise engages your *heart*. Saying "I promise" commits you on a much deeper level than declaring "I have a goal" or even "I'm making a resolution." Think about this: You can *change* a goal, but you can only *break* a promise.

If you're really determined to make a change or achieve something important in your life, start with a promise. Making a promise locks you in emotionally and psychologically. Making a promise makes it clear that failure is not an option. You put your integrity is on the line. Making a promise to someone you care about makes you accountable to someone else in a special way.

If you're like most people, including me, you've set plenty of goals. Take, for example, the goal-setting tradition we call New Year's resolutions. Once a year, millions of people in the United States and around the world earnestly resolve to make positive changes in their lives – from losing weight to starting a new career or writing a book – beginning at the stroke of midnight on January 1st. But far too often, within a few weeks or even days they end up abandoning their resolutions in a fog of excuses and "woulda-coulda-shouldas" and general feelings of disappointment and discouragement.

"You can* change *a goal, but you can only* break *a promise."

A University of Scranton study found that only 8% of people were successful with their New Year's resolutions. That amounts to a 92% failure rate! In fact, the second Friday in January is now called Quitter's Day because that's when about 80% of people have given up on their New Year's Resolutions.

It's almost as if people make their New Year's Resolutions with their fingers crossed behind their backs. Most people seem to realize they're just going through the motions, that they're not serious about reaching the goals embodied in the resolution. This happens, in part, because we don't take the word "resolution" seriously. It's a word without any real power. We're all aware that a resolution is non-binding, like the many non-binding resolutions that Congress adopts every year.

This well-meaning, but often futile, annual ritual inspired American actress and director Joey Lauren Adams – known for her roles in popular films such as "Chasing Amy" and "Big Daddy" – to compose a tongue-in-cheek blessing: "May all your troubles last as long as your New Year's resolutions."

With Adams' humorous observation in mind, I often offer the following unsolicited advice at the beginning of each year: New Year's Resolutions simply don't work. Don't even bother making Resolutions. Instead, I urge people to turn New Year's resolutions into New Year's promises. Why?

Because a promise is more powerful, more binding than either a resolution or a goal.

Perhaps you've experimented with more formal and serious goal setting, maybe reading books on the subject or attending self-help seminars where you've dug deep to determine your goals, declare your objectives, and set out your priorities and intentions. But then what? How many of your important goals have you reached? Again, if you're like most people, it's probably been hit-or-miss.

There's a reason for this, and it's not that you're weak, lazy or hopelessly undisciplined. The reason has to do with what I call "the heart connection." A resolution or a goal, when you get right down to it, is just something you *think* about. What's missing is *feeling*. What's missing is the heart connection. A promise, by contrast, comes from the heart. And a promise goes to the heart when you make a promise to someone you care about, like the promise I made to my mother. Putting your heart into it makes all the difference.

Like Jim Rohn, Jack Canfield and many others, Napoleon Hill recognized the power of promises. The author of the self-help classic *Think and Grow Rich*, Hill stipulated that rather than simply pondering changes we'd like to make, it's essential for us to make a *promise* to pursue our life's purpose and cultivate a burning desire – a passion – to succeed.

Hill believed that making a promise is an essential first step in his self-confidence formula for achievement. Here's how Hill describes what readers should say to themselves in the first of five steps in his success formula:

"I know that I have the ability to achieve the object of my definite purpose in life; therefore, I demand of myself persistent, continuous action toward its attainment, and I here and now *promise* to render such action." [My emphasis]

Hill recognized that a promise propels you in a powerful way toward your goals and dreams. He understood that a promise can replace confusion with clarity, and provide unstoppable motivation, inspiration, and purpose where there had been nothing but unrelenting indecision, doubt, and hopelessness. A promise truly is make-or-break.

During his "What's Your Promise?" interview for this book, bestselling author John Assaraf told me, "We are neurologically wired, I believe, to keep our promises." He went on to say, "There is something uniquely powerful about making a promise that goes beyond traditional goal setting. Setting a promise takes it to a whole new dimension."

Over a century ago, influential New Thought leader Christian D. Larson wrote about the special power of promises and included a series of recommended promises in his 1913 book, "Your Forces and How to Use Them." A slightly edited version of these promises later appeared as "The Optimist's Creed," adopted and distributed worldwide by a global organization called Optimist International. You can read more about Larson and the Optimist's Creed in Chapter 6 of this book, where I have included Larson's promises in "A Promise a Day: 30 Days to a Promising Future." I encourage you to make use of this Personal Empowerment Program (PEP). There's a pep talk in every promise!

PROMISES THROUGH THE AGES - AND MAYBE EVEN IN OUR GENES

The very word "promise" resonates deeply with us on a gut level. Promises have been around since the beginning of time – or at least since the beginning of humankind's recorded history. Some 4,000 years ago, the ancient Babylonians made promises to their gods in exchange for blessings from the gods. At the start of the new year, which in the Babylonian calendar took place in May, the fresh bloom of spring, they engaged in "housekeeping" sorts of rituals like paying old debts and returning items they'd borrowed from neighbors. Their reward, the rituals promised, would be plentiful harvests and other good blessings. Several ancient civilizations sanctified their promises with sacrificial rituals of precious objects and animals – in some cases even venturing into the gruesome practice of human sacrifice.

Fortunately, human beings have evolved to higher ground as more sophisticated civilizations have emerged.

About 2,500 years ago, the Greek philosopher saw promises as a subject worthy of deep intellectual reflection. He offered the view that keeping one's word is a matter of morality and virtue. Above and beyond the important matter of doing the right thing is that of being the right kind of person.

Calling this type of person "the truthful man" in his *Nicomachaen Ethics,* Aristotle described him as a person "who not only keeps faith in his agreements but who is true both in word and in life because his character is such."

Socrates, who was philosophizing in Greece a generation or two before Aristotle, appeared to be thinking along similar lines when he wrote: "The shortest and surest way to live with honor in the world is to be, in reality, what we would appear to be."

In ancient Rome, lawmakers Marcus Tullius Cicero and Gaius Verres also issued the opinion that keeping promises was a moral duty. They took this a step further by formalizing promises through a procedure called the *stipulation*, a series of questions and answers designed to ensure "conveyance" – delivering what one promises:

"Do you solemnly promise conveyance?

"I solemnly promise conveyance."

"Do you promise on your honor?"

"I promise on my honor."

Thomas Aquinas, the 13th-century philosopher and Catholic theologian, proposed the concept of a "natural law" governing promises. Someday he may be proven right, perhaps even at a genetic level, by evolutionary psychology. Researchers in this field are making astounding discoveries about how the people we are today, qualities like how we think and behave and what we believe, might have been shaped by the process of natural selection over a period of eons.

Our capacity for making and keeping promises may play a part in helping us survive and thrive. Promises, evolutionary psychologists point out, are a form of "reciprocity," a "you do this for me, and I'll do this for you" for everyone involved, a win-win. Reciprocity contributed to our ancestors' survival in times of scarcity: "Promise you'll help me slay a wild boar and I promise that our families will share the meat." In modern times, promises like wedding vows encourage relationships that can provide a stable structure for raising children, humankind's future generations.

Our human attachment to promises might even be genetically programmed. Some scientists and philosophers have suggested that we may be born with the mental and moral apparatus required for making and keeping promises, a built-in tool for ensuring that the human race continues to survive and thrive.

THE POWER OF A PROMISE IN THE BUSINESS WORLD

When the London Stock Exchange, today a cornerstone of the world's financial architecture, set out in the early 1800s to establish itself as trusted partner in the burgeoning business of worldwide trading of stocks and commodities, it set its foundations on this motto: "Dictum Meum Pactum" – "My Word is My Bond."

Fast-forward two centuries, and you'll find that integrity is still firm footing for successfully leading a business. Integrity that includes keeping promises.

"Leaders know that honesty and integrity are the foundations of leadership. Leaders keep their promises," wrote Brian Tracy, one of the world's top sales training and personal success authorities, in a blog on his website. "Your greatest personal asset is the way that you are known to others through your professional and personal ethics … your reputation for keeping your word and fulfilling your commitments."

Not surprisingly, research confirms that integrity is a crucial factor in business leadership as well as in the success of business organizations overall. Elizabeth Doty, founder of Leadership Momentum and a recent fellow at Harvard University's Edmond J. Safra Center for Ethics, where she focused on what is required for a business to keep a promise and earn the trust of customers.

"Businesses today make many promises," Doty wrote in an article in the August 2014 issue of "Strategy+Business." "They may promise to deliver value to customers, provide opportunity to employees, deliver growth for investors, or contribute to society by creating jobs, improving public health, providing credit, preserving a free press, or addressing environmental challenges."

Unfortunately, research shows that "many companies struggle to keep their commitments," Doty noted. "Trust in business is low (though higher than trust in government) and broken commitments appear to be a significant cause.

"For example, when asked what CEOs could do to improve trust, 72% of respondents to one survey said, 'Do a better job of keeping your promises.' Another study found that 40% of consumers who had received a promise from a business in a given year felt it was not delivered, and of those, 62% experienced multiple broken promises from that same business."

On a more positive note, Doty also reported that "businesses usually benefit from the trust that comes from promises kept. Several studies show that businesses with a culture of keeping one's word, or with leaders who keep their promises and live their values, are more profitable."

The father-and-son management consulting team of Craig and Jason Womack, in their book, "The Promise Doctrine," presented a compelling case for the importance of making and keeping promises in our personal and professional lives. They wrote: "If you have been looking for the 'key' to personal and professional success, here it is: Make important promises and keep them."

In his foreword to that book, bestselling author and leadership expert Marshall Goldsmith underscored the importance of promise-keeping for all leaders:

"Behind the broad concept of 'ethical behavior' is a simple act that a leader can take to build trust: make realistic promises and keep them. You see, leaders are defined by the promises they make and the promises they keep, and the discrepancy between the two. Leaders who make lots of little (or big) promises they don't keep or who negotiate and who tend to renegotiate without fulfilling their promises will soon find that their people are not following, not listening, not trusting, and chances are, not staying."

I want to share a remarkable example of a business executive who appreciates the power of a promise in the business world. This is a letter to customers from Earl Congdon, Executive Chairman of the Board of Old Dominion (OD), a company in the freight-shipping business. I have highlighted the many references in his letter to "promises." I especially like this statement: "What we're really in the business of doing is keeping promises." Congdon also makes this bold assertion, which is fully in line with the key message of this book: "At OD, we believe the world runs on promises." Amen to that!

CEO's Letter

Old Dominion Customers,

A lot of people think OD is in the business of shipping freight. Managing truck logistics. Moving cargo. And making deliveries.

What we're really in the business of doing is keeping promises.

People keep promises, and that's what everyone who works at Old Dominion does. Because even though it may look like a truck or a drayage container or maybe just a bunch of cardboard boxes, each one contains promises.

A promise that manufacturers will get what they need to produce their product. A promise that retailers will receive the product by a certain date and have it on the shelves. And ultimately, it's a promise that consumers will be able to buy that product easily, whenever they need it.

At OD, we believe the world runs on promises, and no transportation company is better suited or skilled to keep those promises than we are.

The way we keep promises is by continually finding innovative ways to simplify your transportation process. Our four product groups, OD-Domestic, OD-Expedited, OD-Global and OD-Technology, provide you with all the products and services you need to make the promise of seamless simplicity a reality.

OD promises you the power of one source to meet your needs. We are not operating groups or business entities trying to act as one company. We ARE one company. The simplicity that comes from this model empowers us to provide you with complete supply chain solutions both domestically and globally. Our single company structure also allows us to excel on all levels of customer service and ensures that our thousands of employees share the same dedication to you, our customer, each and every day.

Let OD be the company that helps you, and the world, keep promises.

Earl E Congdon

Earl E. Congdon
Executive Chairman of the Board

THE GATES AND BUFFETT GIVING PLEDGE

The Giving Pledge (www.givingpledge.org), created by mega-billionaires Bill and Melinda Gates and Warren Buffett, is a terrific example of wealthy business leaders making a promise that will have profound transformational effects on our world. Through the Giving Pledge, many of the richest people in the world make a promise to give at least half of their enormous wealth to charities. More than 200 billionaires from 30 countries have signed up – including Richard Branson, Ted Turner, and Mark Zuckerberg – promising that hundreds of billions of dollars will be donated to a variety of charities around the world.

As is stated on the Giving Pledge website, this is "a global effort to help address society's most pressing problems by encouraging the wealthiest families to give the majority of their wealth to philanthropic causes … Over the long term, the Giving Pledge hopes to help shift the social norms of philanthropy toward giving more, giving sooner and giving smarter. Signatories to the Giving Pledge are developing innovative approaches to urgent needs such as poverty alleviation, disaster relief, ending human slavery, improving global health and advancing medical research."

A pledge is a solemn promise, one that often is made publicly. Lord Michael Ashcroft, the international businessman, philanthropist and author, wrote the following as part of his public statement when he agreed to participate in the Giving Pledge:

"It is with great pleasure that I make a commitment to the Giving Pledge. I am full of admiration that so many wealthy people have now *promised* to donate at least half of their wealth to charitable causes, either during their lifetime or in their will." (My emphasis)

Dan Gilbert, founder of Quicken Loans, and his wife Jennifer, also made the Giving Pledge. In their public statement, the Gilberts wrote:

"There is nothing more satisfying and exciting than being able to positively affect people and noble causes in this world. Jennifer and I are fortunate to be in the position to join the *promise* and state publicly that the majority of our wealth will be contributed to philanthropy during our lifetimes or after we have left this world."

In that same statement, the Gilberts provided this noteworthy explanation for making this public promise:

"Wealth is created. If that wealth is all passed on to another generation its benefits are often greatly underutilized as those who inherit the wealth view their mission as one of maintaining it. The better path is one that allows wealth to be activated as a force to make the world a better place through endless avenues. The incredible examples of Warren Buffett and Bill and Melinda Gates and their choice to 'activate' their substantial wealth to benefit as many people on this planet in a positive way has served as motivation for others with sizable capacity to also direct their assets in a similar manner.

It is very impressive that they have made this commitment. It is even more impressive that they have done so in the public manner that the *promise* requires because it has taken the formerly hidden world of philanthropy and brought it the kind of visibility and light that will only bring more and more capital to its rightful place of helping to battle the vast number of serious challenges this world faces." [My emphasis.]

I applaud Warren Buffet, Bill and Melinda Gates, Lord Michael Ashcroft, the Gilberts and the scores of other wealthy and generous individuals and families who have embraced the Giving Pledge. They truly are living proof of the transformational impact of harnessing your *PromisePower.*

A WORD OF CAUTION: "WE LIVE IN A WORLD OF BROKEN PROMISES"

When Kate Delaney, the host of the nationally syndicated radio talk show host of "America Tonight," interviewed me a few years ago about the power of making a promise, she opened the show with this sobering statement: "We live in a world of broken promises."

Kate's observation is reflected in a commentary written by a theologian and published in 2014 in "The Catholic Thing" online journal: "Much of our contentment and discontentment arises over the keeping or breaking of promises. Too many lives are filled with broken promises [bringing harm and disharmony to] those who depend on us to keep our promises."

We see evidence all around us that people have grown increasingly cynical, and yet people are hungry for solutions. Millions of people are understandably frustrated about what's happening in Washington and on Wall Street, not to mention in other major political and financial capitals around the world. Day after day, month after month, year after year, we see a sorry spectacle of finger pointing and gridlock.

Some people – maybe you're one of them, as I can be at times – are cynical about promises. We seem to be surrounded by people who make promises but don't keep them. Politicians, for example.

The negative, angry, dark, and pessimistic tone of recent presidential campaigns distressed many observers, including me. Many voters seemed to gravitate toward candidates who inflamed resentments, stoked fear, and spread distrust of the status quo. New York Times columnist David Brooks spoke for many in his column "An Avalanche of Distrust," published two months before the election. "Distrustful politicians were nominated by an increasingly distrustful nation," Brooks wrote. "A generation ago, about half of all Americans felt they could trust the people around them, but now less than a third think other people are trustworthy."

Brooks concluded on a hopeful note, however. The world's great religions and wisest philosophies, he wrote, "have championed the paradoxical leap: that even in the midst of an avalanche of calumny, somebody's got to greet distrust with vulnerability, skepticism with innocence, cynicism with faith and hostility with affection."

In an era that seems to be marked by cynicism, fear and mistrust, the very idea of making and keeping a promise seems almost quaint, a relic from a bygone era when a handshake was a reliable contract, a firm commitment that said, "You can trust me. You can take that to the bank."

Nowadays, many people have the distinct feeling you can't even trust the bank!

I don't want to sound too Pollyannaish here, but to some extent at least, this growing cynicism could be the result of negative, but inaccurate, media bias. We so often hear, for example, that political leaders frequently break their campaign promises. But is that really true? Is it possible that a political leader who breaks a promise gets more media attention than one who keeps a promise?

In the January-February 2012 issue of Washington Monthly, political scientist Jonathan Bernstein noted: "Presidents usually try to enact the policies they advocate during the campaign." Political scientists who have studied this issue over the past 50 years have concluded that political leaders on average have kept, or made a good faith effort to keep, about two-thirds of their campaign promises. This is a surprisingly high percentage. It's certainly not the predominant impression we get from the media.

This is heartening news indeed, quite contrary to popular opinion. I'd like to see more media stories devoted to the many promises kept by our leaders in politics, business, education, civic society and our communities of faith. We might surprise ourselves, and grow a little less cynical as a society, if we focus more on promises kept instead of promises broken.

A key lesson from the Law of Attraction is that we get what we focus on. If we focus on the broken promises around us, we'll get more of that. If we focus on promises made and kept, we'll get more promises made and kept. We should reinforce the expectation that promises should be kept, not broken.

"If we focus on the broken promises around us, we'll get more of that."

MY "MAKE-A-PROMISE" MISSION

If, as Chinese philosopher Lao Tzu stated, a journey of a thousand miles begins with a single step, a promising future for you and the world at large begins with a single promise.

A powerful lesson I took away from the promise I made to my mother is that you may not always know exactly where a promise will lead you. Made with integrity, a heartfelt promise can point you in the right direction without you even knowing the destination. A promise fulfilled can open many unexpected doors. Keeping my promise to my mother turned out to be the first step in an exciting new direction for me as a personal empowerment author, speaker, and coach.

My promise-born book – *HabitForce! How to Kick the Habits of FAILURE and Adopt the Habits of SUCCESS* – has served as the basis of numerous speeches and workshops and as the catalyst for a second personal empowerment book. Embracing my promise-inspired role as a self-help author, a few years later I drew upon my expertise as a speechwriter and speech coach to write *All the World's a Podium*. I encourage you to read more about my approach to public speaking in my book – *The Joy of Public Speaking* (published in 2021). *The Joy of Public Speaking* (an updated version of *All the World's a Podium*) is the first book in my personal empowerment trilogy.

Without delving too deeply into this subject, here's some perspective about my view that public speaking is a key personal empowerment skill. I've always been drawn to something President Kennedy said at a press conference. He was asked whether he enjoys being president. Kennedy said he does, and he cited what he called the ancient Greek definition of happiness: "The full use of your powers along lines of excellence." That profound idea has stuck with me over the years.

I believe speaking to audiences – with confidence, authenticity, comfort, and even joy – is an important skill to develop because it helps us achieve "the full use" of our powers. Which is to say our peak potential. The power of speech, after all, is a distinctly human ability. And yet, studies show that roughly 75 percent of the population – about six billion people worldwide – suffer from some degree of fear, trepidation, anxiety, or even outright terror when it comes to public speaking. That's why I focus on ways to help people make the shift from stage fright to stage delight.

If we fear public speaking, if we shy away from speaking opportunities as a result, we fall short of making full use of our powers as human beings. Failing to find our voice means that we fall short in both self-confidence and self-expression. And that ultimately diminishes our level of personal power and happiness. That's a thumbnail explanation of why I regard effective public speaking as more – much more – than a career booster or a leadership skill.

The book you're reading now – *Harness Your Promise-Power* – is the second book in my personal empowerment trilogy. The third book in the trilogy is coming soon. It's a new and improved edition of *HabitForce!* – titled *Harness Your HabitForce*. These three books and the associated "power tools" – Speaking / Habits / Promises – propel my Triad Empowerment System.

In this book about harnessing your *PromisePower*, I focus on my heartfelt promise to my mother that has evolved into my magnificent mission: to share with you and millions of others the power of making a promise as a gift you give to yourself, as the key to changing your life and transforming the world around you in positive ways.

I'm excited to now be sharing what I have learned from personal experience, research, and a series of "What's Your Promise?" interviews sprinkled throughout the book. I've learned many wonderful things and met many amazing people who have personally experienced the transformative power of a promise in their own lives.

So, it is now my mission to share the power of a promise with millions of people around the world, to bring widespread recognition to this power as a uniquely effective pathway to personal empowerment, goal achievement, and integrity enhancement – and to provide practical steps for harnessing this irrepressible force for good.

In the next chapter, I discuss in detail where this amazing *PromisePower* comes from and how we can begin to harness it and cultivate it in others.

"Promise me you'll always remember:
You're braver than you believe, and stronger
than you seem, and smarter than you think."
– Christopher Robin in A. A. Milne's "Winnie the Pooh"

CHAPTER 2

Ya Promise? It's Not Just for Kids

How we learn about the potent power of promises
Implicit Versus Explicit Promises

ASKING "YA PROMISE?" IS NOT JUST FOR KIDS

Hearing or saying the words "Ya promise?" sends me straight back to childhood. I can't count the number of times I heard them as a kid. Ask a friend to lend me popsicle money, adding "I'll pay you back," and he'd hit me with, "Ya promise?" Tell my brother he could try my fancy new yo-yo in five minutes if he'd just quit trying to grab it from me already, and I'd get, "Ya promise?" And my response, "Yeah, I promise," made it a deal.

You probably hear echoes of "Ya promise?" from your own childhood as well. Looking back at those exchanges as adults, they might sound childish and silly. But that's how we learned a fundamental lesson and put into practice a basic tenet of human civilization: Promises are woven into the cultural fabric of values, ideals and beliefs that keep our society functioning.

Social cohesion depends on an underlying bedrock of trust, as Jack Canfield noted in his foreword to this book. "The act of making and keeping promises comes very close to being a universal value in human society," he wrote. "If people routinely made promises and broke them, if we could no longer trust that other people were going to do what they say, society would fall apart. Chaos would reign."

Telling each other "I promise" as kids kept us on the up-and-up with each other. We sealed particularly serious promises by solemnly reciting: "Cross my heart and hope to die, stick a needle in my eye." "Cross my heart" – a clear reminder of the heart-centered nature of a promise – was accompanied by the ritual marking of a big X across our chest with our finger. The "hope to die, stick a needle in my eye" part made a painful point of the fact that breaking a promise was a big, bad, no-excuses no-no. Violating a promise opened the door to the indignant wrath of *"But you promised!!!"* along with a sinking feeling in your stomach because you knew you let somebody else down. And you knew you let yourself down too.

FROM THE MOUTHS OF BABES: PROMISES MATTER

Research in the field of child development has found that children as young as six have strong ideas about promises. For example, psychologists at Fisher College in Boston did a study with 40 children between the ages of 6 and 10. The children were told stories about people who broke promises and were then asked to judge them for this behavior.

With the intention of determining whether the children would judge certain types of transgressions more harshly than others, the researchers presented stories with a variety of scenarios: There was Sam, for instance, a boy who promised not to take things that did not belong to him but went ahead and stole a quarter from his classmate's desk. And there was Susan, who promised to be more active during recess, but decided to read a book instead. The researchers were surprised by their findings: The children, regardless of the nature of any specific promise, harshly judged whoever made that promise and broke it. The take-away: The very act of making a promise matters. And people don't appreciate it when promises are broken.

The children in this study were onto something that philosophers and ethicists have been discussing for eons.

"Few moral judgments are more intuitively obvious and more widely shared than that promises ought to be kept," notes the online "Stanford Encyclopedia of Philosophy."

Kids seem to know this instinctively, as Ben Moser demonstrated in fulfilling his promise ...

Ben's 4th Grade Promise to Take Mary to the Prom

Ben Moser of Harrisburg, Pennsylvania, was in the 4th grade when he made a touching promise to a classmate with Down syndrome. Ben told Mary Lapkowicz that when he was old enough, he would take her to the high school prom.

Seven years later, even though the young friends had lost touch, Ben fulfilled his promise to Mary.

"He watched over her constantly," their 4th grade teacher, Tracey Spogli, recalled in a story published by the Harrisburg Patriot-News. "If she was looking like she wasn't having fun, he would go over and talk to her. He would pull her into whatever activity they were doing."

The young friends were separated in 6th grade, when Mary switched to the Central Dauphin school district, where her father was a math teacher. He also worked with the Central Dauphin's football team, and Mary began to assist him. Meanwhile, Ben attended school in nearby Susquehanna, and, in high school, he became the quarterback of the football team.

It was at a football game, Central Dauphin versus Susquehanna, when Ben and Mary ran into each other after six years apart. Ben remembered his promise to Mary and the following year, the year of the prom, he presented her with a bouquet of balloons upon which he'd written "PROM." She happily accepted his invitation, and they enjoyed their night together at the high school prom.

And while they don't consider their relationship a romantic one, "I thought Mary was really cool," Ben told the Patriot-News reporter. To which Mary added, "He was sweet."

Linda Moser, Ben's mother, heard about his promise when he made it back in 4th grade.

On prom day, she posted this message on Facebook:

"Today was probably the proudest I have ever been of my son in his lifetime to date! He has grown into a man with a big heart, a deep sense of putting others first, and most of all making people feel special and loved.

"Today," she continued, "with joyful tears in my eyes and down my face I watched a promise made seven years ago to a beautiful girl fulfilled."

IMPLICIT VERSUS EXPLICIT PROMISES

Looking back on my childhood days, I realize that asking "Ya promise?" was a bold thing to do. We didn't think twice about putting other kids on the spot – and sometimes even grownups – by asking someone to follow up statements like "I will" or "I'm going to" with a full-out promise for which they will be held accountable.

But then we grew up, and asking "Ya promise?" fell by the wayside. And that, I think, is unfortunate. In our adult world, words like "I will" or "I'm going to" imply follow-through. In essence, these are implicit promises. But of course, people don't always follow through. I believe that as adults we would do well to ask, "Ya promise?" of our friends, relatives, co-workers and clients when they make implicit promises, as well as of our civic, business, spiritual and political leaders.

Many people who genuinely care about others enlist the power of a promise to make binding commitments, to right wrongs and, ultimately, to create a better world for all of us.

In the historic and masterful "I Have a Dream" speech given by Martin Luther King, Jr., at the Lincoln Memorial during the civil rights march on Washington on August 28, 1963, he admonished the nation to redeem the broken promise of freedom and equal justice for African Americans:

"In a sense we've come to our nation's capital to cash a check. When the architects of our republic wrote the magnificent words of the Constitution and the Declaration of Independence, they were signing a **promissory** note to which every American was to fall heir. This note was a **promise** that all men, yes, black men as well as white men, would be guaranteed the "unalienable Rights" of 'Life, Liberty and the pursuit of Happiness.' It is obvious today that America has defaulted on this **promissory** note, insofar as her citizens of color are concerned. Instead of honoring this sacred obligation, America has given the Negro people a bad check, a check which has come back marked "insufficient funds."

"We have also come to this hallowed spot to remind America of the fierce urgency of Now. This is no time to engage in the luxury of cooling off or to take the tranquilizing drug of gradualism. Now is the time to make real the **promises** of democracy." (My emphasis throughout)

Echoing these promises, President Lyndon Johnson gave a remarkable speech a week after the civil rights protests in Selma, Alabama. In a special address to a joint session of Congress that was televised nationally on March 15, 1965, President Johnson spoke eloquently about "The American Promise" (also known as Johnson's "We Shall Overcome speech.").

This historic speech is well worth reading in its entirety. I will only call attention to a few select passages here. In the speech, Johnson invokes the power of the **promise** of equality and dignity to all Americans … and calls on the country to keep the promise of our nation.

The speech begins with these words: "I speak tonight for the dignity of man and the destiny of democracy. I urge every member of both parties, Americans of all religions and of all colors, from every section of this country, to join me in that cause."

Johnson goes on to explain that America …

"[W]as the first nation in the history of the world to be founded with a purpose. The great phrases of that purpose still sound in every American heart, North and South: 'All men are created equal' – 'government by consent of the governed' – 'give me liberty or give me death.' Well, those are not just clever words, or those are not just empty theories. In their name Americans have fought and died for two centuries, and tonight around the world they stand there as guardians of our liberty, risking their lives.

Those words are a **promise** to every citizen that he shall share in the dignity of man." (My emphasis)

Both consequential speeches refer to what were clearly implicit promises to all people, regardless of race, made in the Declaration of Independence. "We hold these truths to be self-evident, that all men are created equal, that they are endowed by their Creator with certain unalienable Rights, that among these are Life, Liberty and the Pursuit of Happiness." The Declaration does not include an explicit promise that the United States will at once treat all men equally. Nor does the Declaration state that this new nation will uphold these unalienable rights for all men (or women). The institution of slavery existed at the time and there was no mention of abolishing slavery at the dawn of our new nation.

Nonetheless, there was clearly an implicit promise to that effect. And more importantly, many people – many millions – took this Declaration to be a promise of equality for all men regardless of their race.

Martin Luther King and Lyndon Johnson both made it clear that they believed an unrestricted promise of equality and dignity was made. And they endeavored to turn what had been an implicit promise into an explicit promise. I wonder how American history might have been different if enough people had gathered outside Independence Hall in Philadelphia in the sweltering summer of 1776 and challenged the delegates to make the implicit promise of equality explicit by asking a resounding: "Ya promise?"

DORIS KEARNS GOODWIN'S PROMISE TO HER HUSBAND

Let's stay with the 1960s era for another powerful prom ise story. Historian Doris Kearns Goodwin's book, *An Unfinished Love Story: A Personal History of the 1960s*, is the result of a promise she made to her husband, Richard Goodwin. Before his death in 2018, Doris Goodwin promised him that she would finish writing the book they had embarked upon together.

Doris Goodwin explains: "This book began with the 300 boxes my husband, Dick Goodwin, had saved from his time in public service when he worked with John Kennedy, Jackie Kennedy, and Lyndon Johnson in the White House, and with Robert Kennedy and Eugene McCarthy. We began spending our weekends exploring the boxes, reliving the sixties through a veritable time capsule of the major events and the major figures of the era."

Doris Goodwin now says this intensely personal book means more to her than anything she has ever written. I should also point out here that the 33-year-old Richard Goodwin was the White House speechwriter who helped to craft Johnson's "The American Promise" speech in 1965 cited above.

HOW WE LEARN ABOUT THE POTENT POWER OF PROMISES

Jack Canfield said it well in his amazing foreword to this book: A promise is a promise.

The question is: From whence does this unique power of a promise originate? What explains the why a promise – and the word promise itself – is imbued with so much power?

The answer is not easy to discern. It's enigmatic: simple and complicated at the same time. We learn about the power of promises from our families and friends, our schools and places of worship, the communities we grew up in and the larger society that surrounds us. We also learn about promises from books, movies, songs, and other forms of popular entertainment. And the lessons we learned carry on for a lifetime.

First in line with promise lessons were our parents. Given the intense, instinctive connection we share with our parents, the things they do and say in our earliest years seep in and influence us below the level of conscious awareness. These lessons can have lifelong sticking power – for better or worse. The promise I made to my mother shortly before she passed away worked its transformative magic in my life in large measure because I learned about promises from my mother.

It's not as if my mother – or most parents, for that matter – had a strategy or was working from a textbook on promises. The things she taught me were practical and timely, emerging on an as-needed basis in exchanges like this:

"Mom, can I go to Bobby's after school today? He got a new bike and told me I can try it out."

"That sounds fun … but what about your homework?"

"I can do it when I get home. I can only stay at Bobby's till his dad gets home at 5 o'clock."

"Hmmm … all right, you can go. But only if you promise to be home by 5:30 and get to your homework right away."

"I will, Mom. I promise!"

My mother also kept me honest. I knew full well that if I dared to promise her something and not come through, I was in for a stern talking-to at the very least. If my infraction was a big one, I might face dire consequences like not being allowed to watch TV for a week. My young brain also quickly grasped that breaking a promise meant my mother would think twice the next time I uttered the words "I promise."

Can you remember your mother, father or another adult you were close to and some of the things you learned from them about promises? While writing this book, I've spoken to various audiences and had conversations with friends and colleagues about promises. The subject never fails to elicit strong feelings and indelible memories about lessons many people received about promises in their formative years. Among the comments I have received:

- My mother taught me that once I made a promise it's non-negotiable. If I promised I would eat all the peas off my plate at dinner for the reward of dessert, I couldn't later make my scrunched-up 'Ewww! Yucky peas!' face and beg for dessert with a big *'please?!'*"
- My grandma clued me in about making promises I could realistically keep. 'I promise I'll quit throwing my clothes on the floor and will put them in the hamper instead' was a reasonable promise. 'If you let me go to Susie's party, I promise I'll wash the dishes for the rest of my life!' was not.
- My dad showed me by his actions that you stick to your promises no matter who you make them to. It could be a promise he made to my mother that he would clean the garage on Saturday, or the promise I remember him making to a homeless guy who hung out at a bus stop in our neighborhood, telling him, 'Sorry, buddy, I don't have any spare change with me today, but I promise I'll give you a dollar tomorrow.' He always kept his promises and that was a powerful example for me."

If you were a Girl Scout or Boy Scout, you were introduced to the concepts of self-improvement and positive change in the world through a promise. The founders of these organizations carefully crafted a promise to help young people develop qualities like honesty, helpfulness, courage, and character. A Girl Scout promises: "On my honor, I will try to serve God and my country, to help people at all times, and to live by the Girl Scout Law."

Boy Scouts recite a similar promise with the aim of helping boys "be prepared for life," as the organization describes it. One phrase in that promise – "to help other people at all times" – serves as the foundation of a national campaign that honors alumni scouts who make ongoing contributions to helping others and bettering their communities, exemplifying the "promise made as a boy and kept as a man."

Tony Robbins, one of the best-known names in the personal empowerment arena, made a promise as a boy that has reverberated his entire life ...

Tony Robbins' Thanksgiving Dinner Promise

Tony Robbins is a sought-after speaker, bestselling author, financial coach to multimillionaires and the star of the Netflix TV series, "I Am Not Your Guru." But his difficult childhood experiences wouldn't have predicted any of these accomplishments.

The oldest of three children, Tony grew up in the outskirts of Los Angeles with an abusive, alcoholic mother and, essentially, with no father, as his mother married and divorced several times. Day-to-day life was tough, financially and otherwise, for the family. Toughest of all were holidays like Thanksgiving, when a turkey dinner with all the fixings was often out of the question.

One Thanksgiving day, Tony recalled, there was an unexpected knock at the door. A stranger had shown up, with no explanation, to bring them a heaping basket of food. So elated and emotionally moved by this delicious act of kindness, Tony recounted years later, that "I ***promised myself*** that someday I would do well enough to do this for other families." [My emphasis.]

Tony was just 11 years old at the time. In the years since, his promise has put nourishing food on the tables of millions of families struggling to get by, just like his family had been. He began by anonymously giving needy families bags of groceries for Thanksgiving dinner, much like the stranger who came to his family's door.

Tony credits his boyhood promise with changing his life, propelling him to transcend his difficult childhood and become a powerhouse on a mission to motivate others to transform their lives for the better.

As his financial success flourished, he established the Anthony Robbins Foundation. Through its international holiday "Basket Brigade" and year-round programs, the foundation feeds millions around the world. Its mission also extends to improving the lives of inner-city youth, senior citizens, the homeless, and those in prison.

LEARNING TO KEEP OUR PROMISES

A friend of mine, knowing that I was writing this book, told me about how his mother made promises to him that she never kept, leaving him feeling deeply disappointed and hurt. Particularly painful, he recalled, was how she had promised to take him out for a nice dinner when he graduated from high school, and how crestfallen he was when she didn't deliver. His mother's unreliable behavior, he told me, had a profound effect upon him, but a surprisingly positive one: When he became a parent himself, he made a point of assiduously keeping the promises he made to his children, determined to not disappoint them the way his mother had disappointed him.

I learned a lot about keeping promises from my sister, Pattie. Four years older than me, Pattie often filled the role of substitute mom after school when our real mom was still at work. We were latchkey kids before there was a term for it. And to be candid, Pattie was often forced to play the role of a drill sergeant, ordering my older brother, Mike, and me to clean up our rooms, do the dishes, set the table, straighten up the living room, or do our homework *before Mom gets home!* It was a daily, thankless chore for Pattie. Looking back, I wish we had made her life – and my mother's – a little easier by obeying and helping much more than we did.

The three of us had a lot of fun growing up together, but there was no question that Pattie was in charge. She could be very no-nonsense about a lot of things, including the matter of keeping her word. Pattie always kept her promises.

Growing up, I always knew that when Pattie promised something – that she'd meet me outside school and walk me home when I was too little to cross busy streets in San Francisco by myself, or she'd share her Halloween candy with me, or she'd for sure tell Mom if Mike and I didn't stop rough-housing, she meant it. Thanks to Pattie's promise-keeping ethic, I got home from school safely, I enjoyed way too much Halloween candy (and developed the cavities to prove it!) and now and then Mike and I did keep the rough-housing to a minimum. And Pattie could feel good about herself for doing what she promised she'd do.

One promise that my sister made to me touched home, literally, when I was still in high school. For reasons too complicated to go into here, Pattie promised to let me live at her house during my junior year of high school. It wasn't easy for her to provide me with a room to stay in and food to eat, but she never complained, and I was always grateful to her for being so generous and caring. She promised and she followed through, and I'll always love her for that.

Along those same lines, here's an inspiring story about a remarkable woman who feels very good about having fulfilled a life-changing promise she made to herself when she was in sixth grade ...

WHAT'S YOUR PROMISE?

Jin Kyu Robertson's Childhood Promise to Become Somebody

Jin Kyu Robertson was a young girl living what she describes as a miserable existence in South Korea with her impoverished family when she made a promise to herself that *someday she would be somebody*.

That promise would see her go on to earn a Ph.D. from Harvard, with a career along the way as an officer in the U.S. Army while raising two children as a single mom. She has also published a bestselling memoir, "Major Dream: From Immigrant Housemaid to Harvard PhD," and has shared her inspirational story with millions of people in books, media interviews and speaking engagements.

In the sixth grade, Jin learned that her parents weren't planning to send her on for more schooling. They thought elementary school education for girls was enough and expected her to stay at home. "That's when I woke up," she said. "I thought, 'This is totally wrong!' I became a warrior, determined that I was going to become somebody and bring justice to this world."

Lacking any role models for success in her family, she consulted her teacher. "I want to become somebody in the future," she told him, "so what would be considered to be the most success in this world?" He advised her to earn a Ph.D. doctoral degree as an authority in a field of her choice. The path to the Harvard Ph.D. in Asian Studies that she would ultimately earn began with the step of revving up her study habits in elementary school.

"Until I reached sixth grade, I was kind of a dumb little girl … at the bottom of my class," Jin said. "Once I promised myself that I would become a Ph.D., that became my guiding light. Now I was this single-minded girl reaching for that goal."

Driven by her promise, she discovered inner resources that energized her, sharpened her focus and boosted her grades. When she graduated from the sixth grade, she was second in her class academically, and the top girl student in the entire school. She did well in high school, but after graduation she found herself feeling trapped, working long hours at a wig factory. Then she spotted a Help Wanted ad for housemaids in America. She thought this could be the start of the successful life she had promised herself. And so, at the age of 22, with a one-way ticket and $100 and knowing hardly a word of English, she bid her family farewell and boarded a plane to New York City.

The housemaid job she came to New York for had been filled by the time she arrived, so she worked for several years as a waitress. She met a man, married, and had a child. At the age of 28, worn down by domestic violence, she left with her eight-month-old baby girl and enlisted in the U.S. Army as a private. Ten years later, she was U.S. Army Major Robertson, overseeing a platoon in Germany and then assigned to Japan as the Army's liaison to the Japanese Self Defense Forces, the first woman to hold that position. Meanwhile, she pursued her college studies. She retired after two decades in the Army and enrolled at Harvard, where she earned a master's degree in East Asian Studies at the age of 43 and, at 57, finished her Ph.D., focusing on relations among the United States, Korea and Japan.

Jin's memoir, published in 2011, has sold more than a half million copies. She published a second volume in 2013 and is now working on a third volume. For almost a dozen years, she hosted the popular Voice of America/World Talk Radio show, "American Dreams: The Sky Is The Limit."

Jin credits her remarkable success to the promise she made when she was just a little girl. At first, becoming somebody was her dream. But when she promised herself that she would make it happen her life was transformed. The promise turned her dream into action.

And here's an inspiring story of a lifesaving promise that was the result of a tragedy.

Tony McColl's Family and Friends Launch

The Lifesaving "Tony's Promise"

The family and friends of Tony McColl have made a big difference in the lives of countless others. It started with a promise Tony himself made when he proudly got his driver's license at the age of 16. “I will never drink and drive,” he announced to his proud parents, who were thrilled and surprised since they’d never asked him to make such a promise. Tony had come up with this all on his own.

He went on to live that promise, and he encouraged his friends to steer clear of drinking and driving, too. Tony was something of a gentle giant – a tall, brawny football player at his high school in Luskville, Quebec, Canada.

Tragically, on April 16, 2011, when he was just 19 years old, he was killed when a drunk driver, just 20 years old himself, crashed head-on into Tony’s car on a local highway. Just days after his death, Tony’s family and friends channeled their grief and anger into creating a powerful campaign that has inspired thousands to help put an end to drunk driving.

“Tony’s Promise” was launched with a moving video posted on YouTube. The video prompted an outpouring of responses. “I promise!” one person after another declared. A “Tony’s Promise” Facebook group was also formed asking people to honor Tony’s memory by pledging to “never drive or let another person get behind the wheel whilst under the influence.” The Facebook page added: “Every promise made to Tony also goes out to each person who’s been affected by drinking and driving. Every kid, brother, sister, aunt, uncle, mother, father is encouraged to post the name of their loved ones who’ve been killed by impaired driving and even make them their own promise page.”

The Facebook group has grown to more than 6,000 members, among them the Royal Canadian Mounted Police in Nova Scotia. The campaign led to the creation of an “I PROMISE” bracelet. “I wear my bracelet every day,” one Facebook group member posted. “I feel honored when people ask, ‘What is Tony’s Promise?’ and I get to tell them all about this young man, his family and his wonderful friends who are spreading the word and making a difference." Supporters have also created an annual Tony's Promise Music Fest to benefit the Children's Hospital of Eastern Ontario and support ongoing efforts to spread the word.

And Tony's father, David McColl, has created his own one-man campaign in which he makes presentations about drunk driving to a wide variety of organizations, from high school students to parent groups.

"I am honored that I get to speak to groups of people 20-30 times per year about the crash and some of the less attractive details of his death," he said. "I will continue to do this necessary, preventive work if it means a life may be saved and a family, friends and community may be spared the pain that a lot of us have experienced."

THE ROLE OF PROMISES IN STORIES THAT ENTERTAIN, EDUCATE, AND INSPIRE

Real-life promise stories can inspire us all, young and old alike, to dream big and keep our promises. But, as mentioned earlier, we also learn about promises from books, television shows, movies, fairytales and other forms of storytelling that appeal to active imaginations. The use of promises as a plot device is not limited to fairy tales and other children's stories. As you will see in the examples cited in this section, a promise is used to drive the action and drama and supply a character with motivation in many stories, for children and adults. I refer to this frequent use of promises in stories as the "Promise Motif." (Or "Promise Trope.")

The Promise Motif or Trope often goes unnoticed but is nearly ubiquitous in novels, movies and stories of all kinds. I challenge you to start watching movies and reading stories very carefully. In many instances, you will detect there is a promise – sometimes implicit but more often explicit – that sets the action in motion and provides a potent source of motivation for one or more of the main characters. Authors and screenwriters seem to understand that the two magic words – "I promise" – have a special emotional pull on their audiences. A promise in a story touches the heart and often drives the action of the story.

In the Grimm's fairytale "The Frog Prince," for instance, a wise king sets his young princess daughter straight about a promise she made to a slimy frog. The story begins with the princess promising a frog she happens upon in the forest that she'll bring him home to the castle that evening if he will fetch her favorite toy – a golden ball – from a stream she accidentally dropped it in. But when the frog retrieves the shimmering ball, she grabs it and runs off, leaving the dismayed frog behind, crestfallen that the princess had broken her promise.

The next day, the frog shows up at the castle, loudly croaking that he's looking for the princess. When she sees him, she runs to the king and laments that a "disgusting frog" she made a promise to is bothering her. Her father promptly sets her straight: "That which you have promised must you perform," he tells her. "Go and let him in." She dutifully does so, and over the course of their evening together the frog magically transforms into a handsome prince, freed by the princess from a curse that turned him into a frog.

Moral of the story: Keep your promises. This is an intrinsic value in its own right. But as an added fairytale bonus, you might just get a princely reward in the process. So, you just never know what positive good can happen to you when you keep your promises! I often refer to this as a karmic halo effect. Keeping a promise makes good things happen.

In a poignant scene near the end of The Shootist (1976), John Wayne's final movie, J. B. Brooks (John Wayne's character) asks Mrs. Bond Rogers (Lauren Bacall's character) to make a promise. At this point in the film, the audience knows that Brooks – an infamous gunslinger – is suffering from cancer and only has a few months to live. We also know that he's about to face a gunfight against three men who are eager to best the great J. B. Brooks in the movie's climactic showdown. "I want you to promise me something," Brooks asks Bond. "I want you to promise there'll be no questions. No surmises… Promise me… No tears, Bond." She turns away, recognizing the solemnity of the situation, and appears to give the request a great deal of thoughtful consideration. Finally, she turns back to Brooks and says with conviction: "I promise." Relieved, Brooks nods and says: "Thank you."

At the conclusion of Tombstone, Kurt Russel's character, Wyatt Erp, makes the following promise to Josephine Marcus, his love interest in the film:

"I have nothing left, nothing to give you, I have no pride, no dignity, no money. I don't even know how we'll make a living, but I promise I'll love you the rest of your life."

Another Western movie, "Shantee" (1973), contains a powerful promise story. Glenn Ford plays the title character, Shantee. A retired bounty hunter, he makes a solemn promise to his wife, Valerie. In his words:

"Last night I made a promise and I'm going to keep it. I promised I wouldn't leave the Three Arrows [the name of the family ranch] unless it was on ranch business."

In other words, Shantee promised he would not leave the ranch to go off bounty hunting again. That part of his life was a thing of the past. Later he turns to his wife: "Have I ever broken a promise to you, Val?"

Similarly, in the 1998 poker-related film "Rounders," Matt Damon's character, Mike McDermott, declares: "I just can't do that. I've made promises."

These few words capture the essence of the power of making a promise. That power is echoed in this next story. In the 2005 movie, "Three Burials of Melquiades Estrada," a promise made by one of the characters propels all the drama in this tragic and engrossing saga. Estrada's best friend, a rancher named Pete Perkins, promised his friend that he would return Estrada's body to his family in Mexico if he were to die in the United States. Without going into detail, suffice it to say that Estrada is murdered and Perkins (played by Tommy Lee Jones), embarks on a convoluted and danger-filled journey to return his friend's body to his Mexican village. Throughout the film, the message is clear: A heartfelt promise made to someone you care about, in this case to Perkins' best friend, is uniquely powerful. Powerful enough to compel Perkins to risk life and limb to keep his word to his friend.

Similarly, a solemn promise propelled the action of the 2012 box-office hit "The Hunger Games." In the story, the character Katniss Everdeen volunteers to take the place of her younger sister, Prim, in an annual competition that pits a small group of "tributes" against one another in a survivalist fight to the death. Prim asks Katniss to promise that she will try her best to win the competition, Katniss agrees, and the movie's audience is hooked, eager to see if Katniss will fulfill her promise in the face of incredible odds.

In the 2010 remake of "The Karate Kid," the young central characters, Dre and Meiying, exchange heartfelt promises: Dre promises to attend Meiying's violin audition and Meiying, in turn, promises to be there when Dre competes in the climactic Kung Fu tournament. But Meiying's father disapproves of his daughter's friendship with Dre and forbids her to see him again. The father later relents after learning about Meiying's promise to Dre. "In our family," he says, "we don't break promises." As a matter of family honor, the father allows Meiying to attend Dre's competition.

In "Saving Mr. Banks" (2013), Walt Disney (played by Tom Hanks) makes the following matter-of-fact statement about the power of making a promise. "A man cannot break a promise he's made to his kids, no matter how long it takes for him to make it come true." To underscore the message about the sanctity of a promise made, Disney also states: "I have not broken a promise to my two daughters because that's what daddies do."

In "The Fellowship of the Ring," Samwise Gamgee ("Sam") made a heartfelt promise to Frodo Baggins. Frodo had intended to take the Ring to Mount Doom alone. But his close friend, Sam, makes a promise to Frodo that he will not leave his side. He will help Frodo complete the mission despite the risks they will surely face on their quest.

Underscoring the sincerity of his promise, Sam says the following to Frodo: "I made a promise, Mr. Frodo. A promise. Don't you leave him, Samwise Gamgee. And I don't mean to. I don't mean to."

The promise Sam refers to in this passage is the promise he made to Gandalf after Gandalf recruited him to accompanying Frodo on his trek.

"You must take care of him," Gandalf implores Sam. "He is not safe."

"I will, sir. I promise," replies Sam.

This solemn promise captures Sam's commitment to protect Frodo throughout their perilous journey together. And Sam's steadfast loyalty and dedication to Frodo becomes a hallmark of their dangerous trek.

Two promises drive the action in the Academy Award-winning animated feature "Up." Carl Fredricksen, a 78-year-old retired balloon salesman, and his wife, Ellie, had promised each other that someday they would share the adventure of traveling to Paradise Falls in a remote area of South America and building a house there. When Ellie becomes ill and suddenly dies, Carl decides to keep his promise by using thousands of helium balloons to transport their house to Paradise Falls. He inadvertently takes along a young stowaway, a Wilderness Explorer named Russell, and the two become friends. Along the way, they encounter a colorful bird named Kevin who is frantically looking for her lost chicks, and Carl promises Russell that he will help. But Carl's promise to Ellie and his promise to Russell come into conflict, and he is faced with the choice of saving either his house or Kevin. In the end, Carl manages to keep both promises, but not without a great deal of dramatic tension as Carl grapples with a kind of "Sophie's Choice" regarding which of these two heartfelt promises to keep.

We all find ourselves engrossed in stories – whether in books, movies, plays, operas, TV sitcoms, you name it – that feature heartfelt promises at the center of the action. Promises are frequently used as a plot device to drive the action and provide motivation to lead characters along with dramatic tension. We all want to find out whether the character keeps his or her promise. We care about the outcome because the idea of a character keeping – or breaking – a promise grabs our attention and our emotions.

This is especially true of romantic movies, of course, where clear-cut promises transport us to the innocence of love and limitless happiness. Movies like James Cameron's 1997 mega-hit "Titanic," in which Jack (played by Leonardo DiCaprio), a poor artist, and Rose (played by Kate Winslet), born into money, transcend their social differences and fall madly in love. A powerful, motivating promise plays a pivotal role in saving Rose's life. Just before he dies in the frigid water, Jack asks Rose, who is kept afloat on a small piece of wood, to promise him that she will survive, that she will not give up. *"Promise me,"* he says, *"that you'll never let go."* Rose promises, but before long, nearly submerged in the icy water, she drifts into unconsciousness. When she wakes and sees that Jack has died, she is beside herself with such grief and despair that she wants to give up. Exhausted and nearly hypothermic, she almost surrenders, drifting back toward unconsciousness. But then, suddenly, her eyes snap open, a clear signal that she remembers her promise and vows to keep her word to Jack to "never let go." And she keeps her promise for the rest of her very long life. And she holds her enduring love for Jack in a special place in her heart.

In 2010's mind-bending hit movie "Inception," we discover that a promise plays a role in the unfolding story. The leading character, Cobb (played by Leonardo DiCaprio–again) had made a promise to his wife, Mal. At one point in one of Cobb's recurrent dreams, a distraught Mal screams to her husband, "But you promised!" It's a jarring and disturbing memory for Cobb. As the movie proceeds, viewers begin to piece together that this promise to his now-deceased wife is compelling Cobb to unlock the mystery of what happened. Cobb did not want to face the possibility that his broken promise had somehow been the cause of his wife's death.

In the blockbuster global warming disaster movie, "Day After Tomorrow," the main character, played by Dennis Quaid, exclaims at a dramatic moment after catastrophe has struck and all hope would appear to be lost: *"I made a promise to my son and I'm going to keep it!"* This promise becomes a major plot device that drives the action forward. He had promised to find and save his son, and he makes heroic efforts, against improbable odds, to keep his word.

In the inspirational movie "The Blind Side," which won Sandra Bullock an Oscar for Best Actress, a heartfelt promise sets the story in motion. Early in the movie, which is set in Memphis, Tennessee, a character named "Big Tony" says that he made a promise to his mother on her deathbed that he would get his son, Steven, into a good Christian school. In Big Tony's determination to fulfill his promise, Steven, along with Steven's friend "Big Mike" Oher, are admitted into an upscale private Christian school. It is here where Big Mike, a young African American who appears to have a promising career playing football, becomes acquainted with members of the Tuohy family and the story unfolds.

Big Mike, whose father was murdered and whose mother is a drug addict, is welcomed into the Tuohy family when he's 16 years old. The family later formally adopts Big Mike. Another plot-driving promise emerges when Big Mike is being wooed by scores of university football programs from around the country. Bullock's character, Leigh Anne Tuohy, tells him: "I promise that I will be at every game cheering for you" if he accepts a football scholarship from her alma mater, the University of Mississippi (Ole Miss), which was located about 85 miles away in Oxford. Taking her up on her promise, Big Mike accepts the Ole Miss scholarship, where he becomes a college football star and top NFL draft pick. In his career, he played offensive tackle for the Baltimore Ravens, the Tennessee Titans, and the Carolina Panthers.

In the grownup world, promises undergird so much yet don't always feel as dependable as we'd like them to. We fall in love with someone we think we can be sure of, but our hearts have been broken before and we're not so sure after all. We're hired for a new job where the boss says, "I'm not the kind of person who yells at people who work for me," but those very words make us suspicious. We're thinking about putting money into an investment where the guy telling us about it says he can triple our money. And we're suspicious.

If only we could look them straight in the eye and ask, "Ya promise?" We can. And we should. After all, "ya promise?" isn't just for kids. I encourage everyone to ask that question whenever someone tells you they will do something. Just ask: Ya promise? And see what the reaction is. Often people will admit they aren't willing to "promise" to do something or go somewhere. That's good information to have. In other cases, the person might be willing to promise, and that too would be good to know.

In the next chapter, we'll dig a little deeper into the nature of promises, learning that promises can be divided into three main categories depending on who the recipient is. I call this the Three "Who-To's." The next chapter presents a heart-centered anatomy lesson you won't want to miss.

"Promise only what you can deliver.
Then deliver more than you promise."
– Anonymous

CHAPTER 3

Anatomy of a Promise: Three Types of Promises

Three Types of Promises or the Three Who-To's:

- **Promises we make to ourselves**
- **Promises we make to someone we care about**
- **Promises we make to God or a higher power**

In this chapter we'll take a closer look at what I call the anatomy of promises. There are three main types or categories – the three "who-to's" of promises. You'll also find exercises for exploring promises you've made in the past, explorations that will give you valuable insights into yourself and can help guide you as you shape your promise-centered life in the years ahead.

For starters, let's briefly revisit the dictionary definition of a promise: "*To make a promise is to assure someone that one will definitely do something or that something will happen.*"

What parts of this definition are the most important? The *action words* about *doing something* and *making something happen* are certainly key. But look a little closer and we discover that it's the *people words* that drive the action:

"To make a promise is to assure *someone* that *one* will definitely do something or that something will happen."

That *one* making the promise is *you*, of course.

And the *someone* is the person to whom you're making the promise.

Promises are about people and relationships, not just about getting things done. We don't make promises into an empty void. We make promises *to* someone. The getting-things-done power that a promise possesses is a power that's based upon and backed up by our relationships – and this includes our relationship with ourselves.

Every promise forges a special connection between the promise-giver and the promise-receiver. In this chapter, we'll explore these three "who-to's" – three main categories of promises:

- Promises we make to ourselves
- Promises we make to someone we care about
- Promises we make to God or a higher power

Let's explore these three types of promises in more detail.

PROMISES WE MAKE TO OURSELVES

Over the course of our lives, there's a good chance that all of us will make several promises to ourselves, promises of just about every size, shape and degree of significance. These can range from promising ourselves to work hard and get good grades in elementary school to promising to work in a profession where we're contributing to the health and well-being of others.

A promise doesn't have to be big in size to be big in significance. Even the smallest promise is a promise worth making – and keeping – just as the smallest act of kindness is a kindness worth performing. Every small promise made and kept adds to our inner treasure chest of accomplishment, satisfaction, self-confidence, and a sense of personal empowerment and self-worth.

And as I discuss in Chapter 4: Make a Promise, sometimes it's a good idea to start off by making and keeping one or two relatively small promises to help build up your promise-keeping muscles. It's a little like exercise. You should start working out with lighter weights and not try to bench press 200 or 300 pounds right away. Or start doing five or ten pushups a day. Over time, you build up the capacity to lift heavier weights and do more pushups. The same principle applies to promise-keeping.

Steve Maraboli, author of *Life, the Truth, and Being Free,* said it well: "I feel keeping a promise to yourself is a direct reflection of the love you have for yourself. I used to make promises to myself and find them easy to break. Today, I love myself enough to not only make a promise to myself, but I love myself enough to keep that promise"

Sometimes a single promise we made to ourselves starts out with the clear objective of having a tremendous, life-changing impact. Such was the case for me when I was in the eighth grade and promised myself that I would go to college. This was a pretty unusual thing to do, since no one in my immediate family had attended college, and not too many people I knew growing up had gone to college.

In junior high school, a few years after the assassination of President Kennedy, with the Vietnam War and the Civil Rights movement in the news, I started becoming aware of a bigger world out there filled with all sorts of people and ideas and opportunities that sounded exciting to me. College, I somehow surmised, was my ticket to become part of that bigger, more exciting world. With a college education I could "be someone," as I put it to myself when I was 13. Not a

"Mr. Bigshot" kind of someone. I just wanted to be someone I chose to be, rather than someone others expected me to be.

Brimming with youthful idealism, I also saw myself making a difference in the world, having a positive impact, solving problems, helping people. I liked to write, and even in those early adolescent years I was intrigued by President Kennedy's speechwriter I heard about. Someone named Ted Sorensen. I didn't know much about him, but I thought it would be cool to be a speechwriter in government and have an impact on public policy.

(As a parenthetical note, I had the pleasure many years later of having lunch with Ted Sorensen. He was the guest speaker at a gathering of New York-area speechwriters. This meeting took place just a few years before Sorensen passed away. I'm glad I was able to describe to him how he was the person who inspired me to become a speechwriter. He was genuinely moved, I believe, and I felt great being able to share this with him.)

My plans in my teens were big on ambition but short on details. That was okay. I'd figure it out in college. I was clueless as to how I'd get there. I had never even visited a college campus. My family had no money to pay for college. But I went ahead and made that promise to myself – that I would go to college somehow – and that promise helped to set me on the right path, propelled me forward, sent people to guide me, and opened doors for me.

After I graduated from high school, I attended Napa Community College, supporting myself with work-study jobs, including one as an English tutor in the campus Skills Center. I also served as Student Body President. After earning an associate of arts degree, I was able to transfer to the best public university in the vicinity: the University of California at Berkeley. With the help of scholarships, grants and loans, I applied for the university's study abroad program and spent a life-changing year at the University of Lund, Sweden. I graduated Phi Beta Kappa from UC Berkeley with a degree in political science.

The promise I made to myself when I was 13 years old had come to fruition! But there was more: My youthful idealism also found solid footing in my grownup life. Less than a week after graduating from college, I found myself on a plane to Washington, D.C. for a position as paid summer intern on Capitol Hill. When that internship ended, I looked around for a job and soon became a legislative aide to U.S. Congressman Leon Panetta from the Monterey area, working on international relations, defense and education issues and supporting his efforts to improve the lives of the people he represented in his district and the country.

I felt like I was making the positive difference in the world that I'd envisioned and promised myself back in the 8th grade. I later worked as a speechwriter for the Speaker of the House Jim Wright. Along the way, I also served as a Peace Corps Volunteer in Sierra Leone, West Africa.

So yes, sometimes a single promise we make to ourselves has a tremendous, life-changing impact. A heartfelt promise has the power to propel you in a positive direction, and to keep you moving toward that goal even when times are tough and you begin to doubt you'll ever get there. It's important to cling to the reality that a promise kept generates a positive, karmic halo effect.

In her "What's Your Promise?" interview, my friend, Roslyn Franken, told me about a promise she made to herself that grew into more than she could even have imagined ...

WHAT'S YOUR PROMISE?

Roslyn Franken's Promise to Lose Weight

Her promise started out simply enough: Roslyn Franken wanted to lose weight, something she'd been struggling with for years. That she was successful in accomplishing this is only part of her story.

"This one promise," Roslyn said, "was a kick start to a whole new career path, a whole new passion" – the work she does today as an inspirational speaker and author.

Roslyn made her promise the day before her 40th birthday.

"I got on the scale and saw that I was at my heaviest weight ever," she recalled.

That number hit her hard – the culmination of years spent going on one diet after another, only to see herself put on even more weight after each diet ended. The rollercoaster of losing and gaining weight was not only tough on her body but did a number on her self-esteem, especially considering that she was a hard-won cancer survivor. Ten years before, doctors found a tumor growing on the main artery to her brain and diagnosed her with Hodgkin's lymphoma, a form of cancer that attacks the immune system, progressively disabling the body's ability to defend itself.

Roslyn had fought cancer and won. But there she was, facing that shockingly big number on her bathroom scale. A series of questions suddenly raced through her mind. "I remember asking myself, 'How much more weight do I need to gain?' 'How much worse do I have to feel about myself?"

And then came the big question: "What else needs to happen to kick myself into action?" The thing that needed to happen – the thing that did happen – was a promise Roslyn suddenly made to herself.

She recalled: "Seeing that number staring back at me, I said, 'That's it! Enough is enough!'"

She'd fought back cancer and won. Now she was going to fight to win her battle with her weight.

"On that day I made a very big promise," Roslyn recalled. "'I'm going to take better care of me,'" I promised myself. "'I am going to do what I need to do to lose this weight and keep it off in a safe, sensible, sustainable way.'"

This promise, she quickly realized, was different from every other promise she'd put out there about losing weight.

"This time, it was a lifelong promise," Roslyn said, "and with that comes commitment." In all the years she had spent dieting, there had been no long-term commitment. "I was focused on just losing the weight fast and easy like everybody else … that new diet, the magic solution. But it doesn't work."

What's more, this new promise was a heartfelt expression of self-love.

"When you make a promise to yourself," Roslyn said, "you're actually stating that you feel worthy and deserving of keeping that promise as well."

Liberated from her old ways of thinking and excitedly pursuing new ways of taking good care of herself for a lifetime, Roslyn developed an entirely new approach to her life that goes well beyond diets to incorporate tools for living powerfully and positively. The lessons that she has learned, coupled with a deep desire to share her experiences with others, prompted Roslyn to write a book, *The A List: 9 Guiding Principles for Healthy Eating and Positive Living*. Packed with practical tools, personal insights and positive inspiration, her book has helped thousands break free.

"When I started out with this promise, it was not even on the radar that I would be writing a book about this, that I would be helping other people make the same promise to themselves," Roslyn said.

Today, as a sought-after motivational speaker, Roslyn travels around the country as well as abroad to share her "Lighten Up for Good" approach to food and to life. She is also the host of the talk radio show "How to Thrive After 35" and a seasoned media expert who has been featured in newspapers, websites, radio and TV shows around the world.

"You just don't know where that promise is going to take you," Roslyn said. "If you want to make a promise, make it. Make one promise today. That's all you need to do.

MARQUES OGDEN'S PROMISE TO HIMSELF AFTER HIS "ROCK BOTTOM, SPOILED MILK" MOMENT

(https://marquesogden.com/)

[In his own words]

I made a promise to myself after I experienced "my rock bottom, spoiled milk moment!"

In September 2013, I was working as a custodian in downtown Raleigh for $8.25 an hour to support my family after I had to file for Chapter 7 bankruptcy. This was my second job. I had to work from 10 PM until 5 AM every night. On that fateful September 13 morning, as I was about to head home after my shift, I threw some garbage into the trash dump like I always did. It turns out there was a rip on the front side of the *bag which I could not see, and when I threw the bag into the trash dump, almost all of that stinking garbage fell right back on me. I was covered in spoiled milk, rotten meat, and nasty, horrible-smelling filth. Needless to say, that was a very low, humiliating moment for me.*

Once I cleaned myself up, I sat down on the curb and cried for ten minutes straight. I realized at that moment I had no accountability in my life. I was always playing the victim, and I had no inspiration to be anything of substance or do anything that truly mattered. At that moment, I made a promise to myself! I promised at that rock bottom moment that I WAS NO LONGER GOING TO BE A VICTIM. I WAS GOING TO BECOME A VICTOR! I said to myself, "Marques, nobody is coming to save you in your life. Nobody is going to help you get your life back. No knight in shining armor is going to come and get you off this curb and help you get your life back on track! If you want your life back, YOU are going to have to work your butt off to make that happen. It's all on YOU!"

Once I made that promise to myself, I worked extremely hard, became even more disciplined, and stopped making excuses for myself. It took years, but I finally got my life back on track. Making that promise to myself was absolutely the best thing for me in my entire life!

[Author's Note: A former NFL player (2003-2008), Marques Ogden is an inspirational keynote speaker, three-time best-selling author, business coach and consultant, and Founder of Ogden Ventures LLC.]

Chris Cade shared this touching promise he made to himself during our "What's Your Promise?" interview:

"WHAT'S YOUR PROMISE?"

Chris Cade's Promise to Be There for His Son

"My promise was to devote myself to my son, to really be there, to keep him at the center of my life," said Chris Cade, founder of the Liberate Your Life Program.

Chris made the promise when his son was born. When his marriage hit the rocks a couple of years later, he stuck by it. His son was a toddler, and the family was living in Portland, Oregon, where Chris was earning a six-figure income at a leading high-tech company, when his wife told him she wanted a divorce. Determined to mend his relationship and keep their family together, Chris sought help in personal development programs. The things he learned about himself changed his perspective on life and set off a chain reaction of unexpected events, including leaving his job and getting a divorce after all.

And his promise to his son to be there for him, to keep him at the center of his life, got tricky. Ultimately, it would have serious implications for his career and life decisions. To ensure that Chris could be with his son as much as possible, he and his ex-wife worked out a co-parenting arrangement. But then she informed him that she was moving with their son to Texas. Chris decided that no matter what, his son's well-being would remain his number one priority, and he and his ex-wife worked out an agreement that Chris would also move to Texas and live nearby. When she moved again, Chris moved again – not just once but several times, relocating from one state to another.

As Chris learned from this experience, sometimes keeping a promise can pose enormous challenges. But his heartfelt promise, sincerely given to the son he dearly cared upon, helped Chris persevere and overcome obstacles that came his way.

The promises we make to ourselves are actually very powerful expressions of the regard we have for ourselves. I'm not referring to ego-driven narcissism. What I'm talking about is healthy self-regard in which we recognize, respect and embrace the unique individuals we are. Self-caring helps make us whole and lights our path through life. In the words of the brilliant comedienne Lucille Ball, who was also a very sharp businesswoman, "Love yourself first and everything falls into linc."

WHAT'S YOUR PROMISE?

Barbara Kilikevich's Promise to Find Her Sister

As young girls, Barbara Kilikevich and her sister were separated by adoption. Many years later, when Barbara was about 21, she made a promise to herself: One way or another, she would find her sister.

It wouldn't be easy. With few clues as to where to begin, she relied on persistence and patience as she explored one possibility after another, only to end up at yet another dead end.

Then, in 1995, a burgeoning new technology called "the Internet" – which until then could be accessed only by universities, government agencies and other "official" organizations – became available to the public. Barbara got herself connected and discovered a whole new world of possibilities for finding her sister. But her online searches proved slow-going as well, until one day she had a sudden "intuition hit," as Barbara put it. Going online, she found a group called Search Angels. One thing led to the next and the organization eventually located her sister, six years after Barbara made her promise.

The two long-separated sisters now enjoy a close relationship, even though they remain separated by geography – one of them lives in Florida and the other in California. And Barbara has the deep satisfaction of knowing that a promise she made to herself helped make it happen.

Here's another example of the profound effect a promise to yourself can have on your life.

WHAT'S YOUR PROMISE?

Grace Redman Makes a Promise to Her Own Health and Wellness

(https://www.daretoachieve.com/)

[In her own words]

I have made many promises to myself over the years, but the most profound one came recently. In 2022, I was diagnosed with cancerous growths on my thyroid and had to undergo a total thyroidectomy. My naturopath warned me that I would never be the same again, that my health would decline, and that I would probably gain a lot of weight. In my head, I thought, "Do you know who you are talking to?" I promised myself that I would rise again and that my health would not decline. I committed to my emotional, mental, physical, and spiritual fitness. No one was going to limit me or the vision I had for myself.

Today, at 54, I am grateful to share that I am more emotionally, mentally, physically, and spiritually fit than ever before. The promise I made to myself and my personal transformation as a result have given me a new passion and drive to help others rise above their own perceived limitations.

[Author's Note: Author of *Can I Live?!*, Grace Redman is the founder of Dare to Achieve. She is a success and transformation coach and owner of one of the most successful employment agencies in the San Francisco Bay Area in California.]

WHAT'S YOUR PROMISE?

Victor Garcia's Promise to Make His Wife Feel Loved and Appreciated

[In his own words]

About fifteen years into my marriage, I told my wife that something had to change. We needed to go to counseling because I did not want to be in our marriage anymore, and we needed to work things out. With counseling and a lot of self-reflection, I realized the problem was my own creation. I simply wasn't putting the work into making it a wonderful relationship.

So, I made a promise to myself that I would make my wife feel loved and appreciated every single day.

To do that, I gave myself the "I love you because" challenge. Every day for about a year, while she was sitting in her chair in our home office, I'd kneel down in front of her and say, "I love you because..." and I would fill in the blank. Nowadays, I don't do the "I love you because" statement as often as I used to. But I had established the habit of being grateful for her. This trained me to go into her office each day (which I still do to this day) to show her love and appreciation.

Fast forward about ten years, and our relationship is truly amazing. Being able to say with total confidence that I've become her dream man is, and always will be, my greatest accomplishment. And it all started with the promise I made to myself more than ten years ago.

[Author's Note: In Victor Garcia's own words, he is an amazing husband, serial entrepreneur, and business growth expert. https://www.eightfigureempires.com/]

Where do you stand when it comes to making promises to yourself? Find out in the following Inward Bound exercise, the first of a series of powerful visualization exercises in this chapter and the next to help you get to know your promise-making self a little better.

I suggest that you first read through the entire exercise for an overall sense of the process. You'll want to pull out your Promise Journal to make notes on insights, feelings and anything else that comes up for you during this exercise. If you prefer, you can keep notes on your smartphone or another digital device, but there's something about writing them down on paper that helps keeps you more closely connected with your inner process.

INWARD BOUND

Explore a Promise Made to Yourself

Sit or lie down in a comfortable, quiet place where you won't be disturbed for about 30 minutes. Close your eyes. Take three to five deep, relaxing breaths, in and out slowly.

Recall a promise you made to yourself. It could be a small promise that you made and kept easily, or it could be a big, ambitious promise that led to dramatic, life-changing results. Or it could be something in between.

Think back to what prompted you to make this promise. What was going on in your life and how did you feel about it? Maybe, like Roslyn Franken, you came face-to-face with a painful truth about yourself and felt frustrated and frightened.

Now try to recall the process of making your promise:

- Did you spend some time thinking about it, or did your promise spring into your mind suddenly and maybe even fully formed?
- What was the wording of your promise, and did you say them silently to yourself, speak them aloud, or write them down? Perhaps both.

Revisit the feelings you experienced when you made your promise to yourself. Did you feel happy, excited and motivated? Possibly you felt pressured, worried or something else along these lines.

Finally, consider how your promise turned out:

- Did you keep your promise to yourself? What impact has this had in your life and in the lives of others? And how do you feel about keeping your promise?
- Maybe you didn't keep your promise to yourself. What prevented you from keeping your promise? Don't beat yourself up over this; simply gather information that could help you in the future. What impact did not keeping your promise have in your life and in the lives of others?
- How do you feel about not having kept your promise? Again, no self-criticism here, just observe your emotions about it and gather information.

As you conclude this exercise, slowly return your awareness to the room you're in and open your eyes. Chances are good that you had some fresh and perhaps even surprising insights about promises you've made to yourself. Make notes about them in your Promise Journal to "lock in" their lessons to you and serve as useful information in the future. You might also want to start thinking about a new promise you'd like to make to yourself.

PROMISES WE MAKE TO SOMEONE WE CARE ABOUT

When we make a promise to someone we care about, we are connecting with that someone on a heart level, a feeling level. The feelings we have for them automatically propel us in the direction of keeping our promise. The promise I made to my mother falls into this category.

Of course, the "someone we care about" to whom we make a promise may not always be a beloved parent, grandparent, sibling, spouse, child, some other close relative or a dear friend. "Someone you care about" is an intentionally broad category. It could be virtually anybody. It could even be someone you were close to who has passed away and your promise could be meant, in part at least, to honor that person's memory or your special relationship to that individual. The key here relates to the degree of your heart-connection with the person to whom you make a promise.

Parents' feelings for their children and vice-versa can be profoundly deep. Then there are warm and fuzzy romantic feelings for the "special someone" in our lives. And for friends and colleagues, we have appreciative and respectful feelings. Regardless of degree, feelings are feelings, a level beyond the intellectual or cerebral.

When we make a promise to someone we care about, the promise becomes anchored in a special emotional bond. You naturally don't want to disappoint him or her, and this reinforces your determination to keep your word, to do what you promised. The promise I made to my mother carried the seeds of its own fulfillment by the very nature of our close bond.

Why not make a promise as strong as possible? Why not leverage the power of a promise by making it to someone you care deeply about, someone whose opinion matters a great deal to you? As I have discussed elsewhere, if you have an important goal you'd like to achieve, why not turn that goal into a heartfelt promise to someone you care about? You'll be much more likely to follow through.

A friend of mine told me about the promise he made to his kids that enabled him to finally quit smoking. A heavy smoker since high school, he'd repeatedly vowed to quit, from making New Year's resolutions to staring at himself in the mirror and saying, "Okay, buddy, this is it, I quit!" He would quit for a while, but it never lasted. In his mid-30s, he started experiencing shortness of breath and coughing fits. "That was my wake-up call," he told me. "I could see I was headed in the direction of shuffling around hooked up to an oxygen tank if I didn't stop smoking once and for all."

Finally, instead of *trying to* quit he made a promise that he was *going to* quit smoking and stay quit. And instead of directing that promise to himself, he made it to his two teenage sons.

"I sat them down and said, 'I'm making a promise to you to quit smoking once and for all.'

I didn't actually expect much of a response, but they started telling me how worried they'd been about those coughing fits and my health and all. And my seeing how much it meant to them helped me keep my promise then and continue to keep it today, 10 years later."

Sometimes a promise we make to a loved one can impact our lives in profound ways, as was the case with Todd Newton ....

WHAT'S YOUR PROMISE?

Todd Newton Promises to Make His Grandmother Proud (https://www.toddnewtononline.com/)

In my "What's Your Promise?" interview with Emmy Award-winning television personality and game show host

Todd Newton, he shared the story of his heartfelt promise to "Nana"– his grandmother, Eleanor Kruse – as she lay dying in a hospital.

That promise has guided his course in creating his hugely successful career in TV and much more. Newton is a familiar face to millions as host of Hub Network's "Family Game Night," the Game Show Network's "Hollywood Showdown" and "Whammy!: The All New Press Your Luck," to name just a few. He was also a regular host for more than a decade on "E! Entertainment Television," where he brought viewers face-to-face with Hollywood's biggest stars on the red carpet of major award shows.

Newton considers his Nana to be the most important person in his life, inspiring and encouraging him as he was growing up in St. Louis, Missouri. His grandmother also apparently passed on some of her "entertainer genes" to him: She performed as a comedienne in the St. Louis area during World War II.

Newton was in his early 20s, just getting started in his career, when his beloved grandmother developed a terminal illness. During our interview, he recounted with deep emotion the day he went to visit her in the hospital, knowing that this would be the last conversation he would have with her:

"I bent down, kissed her forehead and said, 'I promise to always make you proud of me.' She smiled. The next day she was gone."

Newton told me that this promise was "the most important thing I have ever done, or said, or ever will commit to in my life. It literally has changed my life for the better."

Talking about this promise some 17 years later is still an emotional experience for Newton, who became choked up during the interview.

To this day, Newtown continues to fulfill his promise to always make his grandmother proud, not just in his entertainment career but in inspiring and helping others. He travels the country giving inspirational speeches about personal achievement and success to university students, corporate leaders and other groups. He has published a memoir, "Life in the Bonus Lane: A Game Show Host's Guide to Success and Fulfillment."

Newton is also the founder of The Newton Fund 4 Kids, which provides state-of-the-art pediatric health care to children in need, and he serves as is the Soul Ambassador for Soles4Souls, an international organization that collects and distributes millions of pairs of shoes worldwide.

Todd Newton's Nana would be very proud of her grandson!

Here's another example of what can happen when you make a promise to someone you care about.

Scottish Singing Sensation Susan Boyle's Promise to Her Mother

In 2009, a shy, middle-aged woman named Susan Boyle, stepping onstage at "Britain's Got Talent," astounded a team of skeptical judges and a television audience of millions when she belted out a beautiful rendition of "I Dreamed a Dream" from "Les Misérables." What propelled her – she was 47 years old at the time and, as she innocently put it, had "never been kissed" – to engage in such a bold act? A promise.

"This was a promise that I'd made to my mum – that I'd do something with my singing," Susan said in an interview later. "She was the reason I pursued my singing. I'm … putting my promise into practice."

Susan's promise was really to herself. In her heart of hearts, she must have known knew she had enormous talent that demanded full expression. Right then and there she could have set a goal of becoming a world-famous singer who sells millions of CDs and attracts millions of fans to sold-out concerts around the world – which is, of course, exactly what happened. But instead, she made a promise to her mother. Although her mother died shortly after that, Susan's promise empowered her to overcome a lifetime of fear and shyness and nearly a half-century of hiding behind other singers in a choir. The power of the promise to her mother made it possible for Susan to blast through intimidation and doubt that could easily have overwhelmed her. But she cared so much for her beloved mother that she was determined to honor the promise.

Stefania Lucchetti (https://stefanialucchetti.it/en/) made a life-changing promise to her grandmother, the fulfillment of which expanded her career as an international corporate attorney into the realm of teaching business leadership and productivity skills.

After Stefania became an attorney, her grandmother asked her not to forget that her real passions in life were to be a writer and a performer. Stefania promised her beloved grandmother that she would find a way to pursue those passions.

Stefania has kept her promise by bringing writing and performing into her work as an attorney. Licensed to practice law in three jurisdictions – Italy, the United Kingdom and Hong Kong – Luchetti is the bestselling author of several books, among them *Ideas in Reality: Making Your Ideas Happen* and *The Principle of Relevance: The Essential Strategy to Navigate Through the Information Age.* She channels her passion for performing into presentations about leadership and entrepreneurship to Fortune 500 companies and as a professor at Politecnico di Milano Graduate School of Business in Milan, Italy.

"The promise I made to my grandmother was always there," she said. "I knew she would be happy that I kept my promise to her."

A remarkable promise that Tara Taylor (https://taratay-lor.ca/) made also reflects the profound power of making a promise to someone you care about. Some years ago, Tara's friend and mentor became ill with cancer. Before her friend passed away, Tara promised that she would pay for the college education of her mentor's sons.

This promise, Tara said, has been one of the driving forces behind her ongoing efforts to be of service to others through writing books, speaking and consulting. Knowing she needed to bring in additional income so she had the financial resources available to keep her promise, Tara has really put herself out there. Her success and determination in pursuing her business goals stem in large part from the promise she made.

Patti Wood made a promise to a friend that proved heart-wrenching for her to keep, even though she knew it was the absolute right thing to do …

WHAT'S YOUR PROMISE?

Patti Wood's Promise to Let Her Best Friend Go

(https://www.pattiwood.net/)

Patti Wood is an international speaker, trainer and the author of *SNAP – Making the Most of First Impressions, Body Language, and Charisma* and other books. During a "What's Your Promise?" interview with me, she recounted the very moving promise she made to her best friend, Roy, and the promise he made to her before he passed away from AIDS.

When Patti and Roy met at college during a freshman orientation session, it was friendship at first sight.

"I looked across the room and I saw this tall, Nordic blond leaning against a grand piano," Patti recalled. "I im mediately thought, 'Oh my gosh, there's my best friend!' I just knew it.

They developed a deep friendship, taking classes together, enjoying each other's company, having fun prompted by what Patti described as Roy's wonderful silliness.

"We were incredibly close," she said, "but as good friends, not romantic, because Roy was gay. "We were like twin souls."

After college, Patti headed to Florida State University, where she earned a master's degree in interpersonal and organizational communication and was invited to join the faculty. Roy became a social worker and moved to Atlanta. Despite the geographic distance, they stayed in close contact by phone and visited each other frequently.

It was during a visit with Roy in Atlanta that Patti learned she was going to lose her best friend.

"We were walking in Piedmont Park, a beautiful park with a lake. He turned to me and said, 'Patti, I am dying of

AIDS,'" Patti recounted. "I just screamed. I remember that the scream reverberated across the lake."

Almost immediately, Patti decided to move to Atlanta and take a job as a temp so she could help take care of Roy. He'd been diagnosed with full-blown AIDS, and his condition deteriorated rapidly. Making things even worse, Patti said, was the stigma attached to the disease – this occurred early in the history of AIDS, when ignorance about how the disease was transmitted was rampant. In fact, when Patti's boyfriend learned that her friend Roy had AIDS, he broke up with her, afraid that he might "catch it" too. Many doctors and other medical professionals were reluctant to treat people with the disease.

As Roy grew more ill, he became unable to eat and was connected to a feeding tube. Suffering from intense pain, he was hooked up to painkillers intravenously.

Knowing that his time was short, he initiated a conversation with Patti that led to their promises to each other.

Patti recalled: "We held hands, and he said, 'Patti, if I decide to let go, to unplug these IVs that are giving me sustenance, will you be able to bear that? Will you be able to let me go?'"

"That was such a hard conversation," she said. "I was so young – in my 20s – and we were so close that I could not see a life without him. I knew it was very difficult for him to make that request, because he didn't want to put me through any pain. He did it very bravely."

"I said, 'I promise you that I will let you go,' that I wouldn't insist that he be revived, wouldn't go to herculean efforts to sustain him if that's not what he wanted.

"But" she added, "I did exact a promise from him: that he would please say goodbye to me before he left.

When a work-related trip became necessary for Patti, she wrote Roy a letter before she left.

"I told him I loved him, and that if he was holding on because of me, it was okay if he let go," she said. "And while I was gone, he unplugged his IVs.

Roy lived for two weeks after that. Patti rushed back to Atlanta to be with him and his family who had gathered around him.

"I was able to share my promise to him with his family, and they honored that promise, which was extraordinarily difficult for them," she said.

And Roy honored his promise to tell Patti goodbye. She had left his side for a few hours when his family contacted her. Roy was calling for her, they told her. When she arrived, he was drifting in and out of consciousness.

And then, "We thought he was gone … but he actually came back," she said. "He came back to make sure to keep his promise to say goodbye."

WHAT'S YOUR PROMISE?

Michael's Life-Changing Promise to His Wife

[In his own words]

I had an amazing, loving home life as a child with devoted parents. When I was fourteen, our family moved from the Charlotte (North Carolina) area to Orlando (Florida) due to my father's job. That's where my journey really began. I was in my last year of middle school and was suddenly the outsider. Not only that. I was also a country boy thrust into the land of Mickey Mouse. There were no accents and everyone else seemed to sound the same. Except me. I was made fun of, and it was a first for me as I was well-liked in school up to this point.

My journey through school would have its ups and downs and would not end favorably for me as I failed my only class my senior year, which meant I could not graduate with my class. Out of stubbornness, I chose not to go to summer school for a measly few weeks to complete my degree and continued to spiral downward. I would go on to complete my high school degree, but it would not fix what was ailing my inner spirit.

Looking back on my life, I believe one of my biggest faults was the inability to ask for help or to simply talk to a friend about my issues. This would all culminate on a sunny day in February 1998 when I attempted to end the pain. I began taking pills that day and simply lost count. I woke up in the back of my parents' car; they simply came out of nowhere, and we were speeding to the ER as they were on the phone talking with their pharmacist friend about what to do. I would go through much counseling and begin to recover.

Just a short month after this frightening incident, I would meet the woman who would later become my wife. During our courtship, we would discuss why I felt the need to do what I did. Soon, I made a promise to her that I would never allow myself to get in that position again, that I would do whatever it took – by focusing on her, my God, my family, my career – whatever I needed to avoid taking such a drastic step.

Since I made that promise, my life has dramatically changed. My wife and I have been married twenty-six years in May (2025). We have two adult children and two very spoiled grandchildren. I just semi-retired as a healthcare executive for one of the largest healthcare systems in the world. I'm now consulting in the same industry.

One of the bright spots in my life – which happens to be the brightest – has been becoming and living my life as a devout Christian. I'm an ordained minister now, and I love serving and helping people. I have a speaking coach and am beginning to make appearances on podcasts so I can help others who are struggling. I know what it's like. I hope my experience – including making a life-changing promise and embracing my deep religious faith – will be helpful to others in their hour of need.

MAKING A PROMISE TO SOMEONE YOU CARE ABOUT... TO KEEP A PROMISE TO YOURSELF

Sometimes we make promises to others as a way of helping us keep promises to ourselves by reinforcing or amplifying our level of commitment. Making a promise to someone you care about means that an important "somebody else" is now directly engaged and involved in helping you keep your promise. And that can be a good thing.

What's not so good is making a promise to someone else just because they want you to make that promise. For instance, don't promise to lose weight or quit drinking or smoking simply to please someone else. It's not going to work. Your motivation will likely fizzle out, and you could end up resenting the other person and the promise is likely to backfire.

Here's an example of what I mean: A friend of mine told me about how, many years before, her boss kept urging her to lose weight, telling her that she was a beautiful woman and wasn't doing herself justice by carrying around an extra 20 pounds.

"It wasn't that he had any kind of romantic interest in me nor me in him," she recalled. "I *wanted* to lose weight, and although he wasn't presenting it in the most tactful way, he was genuinely trying to be helpful." Eventually, she decided to go for it. She promised her boss that she would lose those 20 pounds, by Christmas, still several months away. Thrilled, her boss gave her a thumbs-up ... and then proceeded to check on her progress on a weekly basis. You can probably guess how her weight-loss efforts went: She went on a rollercoaster ride of determinedly dieting and then slacking off and gaining all the weight back. By Christmas she was right back where she started.

That's when she came to a sudden realization: "I didn't want to lose weight for him or anyone else. I wanted to lose weight for *myself*." She changed her who-to, promising herself that she would lose those 20 pounds and keep them off. And voila! She kept her word and has stuck to her no-more-extra-20-pounds promise ever since.

In this instance, my friend demonstrated that she really did care about herself. So, making a promise to herself carried enormous weight, much more than making the promise to her boss. I believe if you make a promise to someone you care deeply about – and that someone can, in fact, be you – you're much more likely to follow through. Here's a great example.

WHAT'S YOUR PROMISE?

Tom Johnson's Promise to His Mother

A few years ago, a friend of mine named Tom Johnson made a promise to his 85-year-old mother. He knew at the time that 'her end was near,' as he described it. He also knew that she was worried about him. He had health issues of his own, having been overweight for years. He also admits that he had a serious drinking problem for a long time.

With a great deal of determination, Tom was able to lose 110 pounds. He stopped drinking completely. And he became an avid pickleball player to stay active and keep in shape. So, he decided to make this heartfelt promise to his ailing mother not long before her passing:

"I promise you, Mom, that I shall stay fit for the rest of my life."

Tom knew that this promise to his mother would be especially meaningful, that it would reassure her that her son would be okay, that he would not regain the pounds he had shed, that he would remain sober. The promise also did something else. It has bolstered Tom's own sense of personal empowerment. Making and keeping a heartfelt promise to your mother is an excellent win-win for both parties.

I also believe it's possible to inject additional punch and power to your promise if you make it on Mother's Day. As I suggest elsewhere in this book, why not give your mother flowers and a heartfelt promise on Mother's Day? A promise like the one Tom made to his mother could be an especially meaningful thing to do on Mother's Day. I suggest it could be a wonderful way to enhance the emotional meaning we associate with Mother's Day if we establish a new tradition of making a promise to our mothers on this special occasion. The same idea applies to Father's Day.

Where do you stand when it comes to making promises to someone you care about? Find out by doing the following visualization exercise. As with the Inward Bound exercise earlier in this chapter, I suggest that you read through all the instructions first to get an overall sense of the process. And pull out your Promise Journal to make notes on insights, feelings, and anything else that comes up for you during this exercise.

INWARD BOUND

Explore a Promise Made to Someone You Care About

Sit or lie down in a comfortable, quiet place where you won't be disturbed for about 30 minutes. Close your eyes. Take three to five deep, relaxing breaths, in and out slowly.

Recall a promise you made to someone you care about. This could be a friend or loved one. It could be a small promise that you made and kept without much effort, or it could be a big, ambitious promise that led to dramatic, life-changing results. Or it could be something in between.

Think back to what prompted you to make this promise. What was going on your life and how did you feel about it? Why did you make this promise? And why to this particular person?

Now try to recall the process of making your promise:

- Did you spend some time thinking about it, or did your promise spring into your mind suddenly and maybe even fully formed?

- What was the wording of your promise? Did you use the words "I promise" And did you state your promise directly to that person? Did you write the words down? Perhaps you did both.

Revisit the feelings you experienced when you made your promise. What feelings did you have for the other person, and what feelings did you have for yourself?

Finally, consider how your promise turned out:

- Did you keep your promise to this person? What impact has this had in your life and in that person's life? How did you feel about keeping your promise, and how did the other person feel?
- Maybe you didn't keep your promise. What prevented you from doing so? Don't beat yourself up over this; simply gather information that could help you in the future. What impact did not keeping your promise have in your life and in the other person's life? How did you feel about not keeping your promise, and how did the other person feel? Again, no self-criticism here, just observe your emotions about it and gather information.

As you conclude this exercise, slowly return your awareness to the room you're in and open your eyes. Make notes in your Promise Journal to "lock in" your insights from this exercise. You might also want to start thinking about a new promise you'd like to make to someone.

PROMISES WE MAKE TO GOD OR A HIGHER POWER

Sometimes we feel moved to make a promise to God or some form of a higher power. It's fair to say that these promises can be considered the most serious and potentially the most binding promises we can make. You can't exactly set a goal to God, but you can make a promise to God.

This is not to say that promises you make to yourself or to someone you care about should be taken lightly. It's merely to point out that the very word promise is imbued with a spiritual connotation and, as such, a promise is bolstered by this special quality.

In the Bible, the Book of Ecclesiastes 5:4-5 states: "So when you make a promise to God, don't delay in following through, for God takes no pleasure in fools. Keep all the promises you make to Him. It is better to say nothing than to promise something that you don't follow through on."

With that admonition in mind, let's recall the promise that Jack Canfield described in the foreword to this book as a "very personal and sacred promise I made to God one night in a darkened apartment when I was 27 years old. Far beyond a goal, it was a promise of how I would live the rest of my life. It was, I realized many years later, a sacred oath to fulfill my soul's purpose, to fulfill my destiny.

"That night I made a promise that literally changed the course of my life. I promised I would spend the rest of my life learning and teaching others about wisdom and love … That promise made many years ago in a darkened apartment in Amherst, Massachusetts, has proven to be a promise that has led to a life more productive, impactful and fulfilling than I ever could have imagined when I was 27 years old."

Note that Jack doesn't explain his concept of God. He doesn't have to. His specific concept could be very different, in fact, from your or my concept of a God or higher power. It doesn't much matter as long as he has positive feelings – feelings of love and reverence – for his God and he is confident that his God has positive feelings for him. And while he was asking for God's help and support, no doubt Jack understood on a deeper level, as we all should understand, that God's work here on Earth must truly be our own. We are the ones who need to take action to fulfill our promises to God.

Alcoholics Anonymous (AA) and related recovery groups usually share an assumption that traveling the road to recovery is a whole lot easier with the help of a higher power. This assumption is set out in the first three steps of AA's 12 Steps:

Step 1: We admitted we were powerless over alcohol – that our lives had become unmanageable.

Step 2: Came to believe that a Power greater than ourselves could restore us to sanity.

Step 3: Made a decision to turn our will and our lives over to the care of God *as we understood Him*.

But, interestingly, AA groups don't require that their members believe in God, let alone believe in any particular God. Over the course of its 90-year history – since its founding in Akron, Ohio, in 1935 – AA has reached people in all corners of the globe, people of every possible religious belief and spiritual leaning – including those with no such leanings at all. Some AA members consider the AA fellowship as a whole or their one-on-one AA "sponsors" as a form of "higher power" that helps keep them accountable and provides encouragement and support.

The key concept is belief in a higher power – something larger than oneself, more powerful, capable of helping us out of problems we're having, from addictions to job crises to relationship difficulties – in a way that we as mere individual human beings might not be able to.

Making a promise to a higher power is sort of a saintly barter system in which you offer something of value to a higher power and, as quid pro quo, that higher power will step in and lend you support, no matter how dire the situation. AA members are encouraged to "turn our will and our lives over to the care of God as we understood him" for which, in return, that "Power greater than ourselves could restore us to sanity."

A promise to God calls in divinely powered reinforcements that can make miracles happen. This point is illustrated by the promise made by Lisa Nichols, who was featured in Rhonda Byrne's "The Secret." Three decades ago, Lisa was a struggling single mom to an eight-month-old son, barely getting by on public assistance and with a total of $12 in her bank account when she made a promise to God.

"I got on my knees, and I said, 'God, if you bring me through this, *I promise* I will spend every moment, every breath, supporting and encouraging others to do the same."

Lisa was asking for God's help while also committing herself to helping others, a commitment she has fulfilled with such determination that today she is a sought-after motivational speaker, bestselling author and millionaire entrepreneur.

Bestselling author John Assaraf made a promise to God on the day each of his two sons was born. He revealed the details of his deeply felt promise for the very first time during his "What's Your Promise?" interview for this book…

WHAT'S YOUR PROMISE?

John Assaraf's Promise to God When His Sons Were Born

As John and I started to talk about his promise story, I could tell right away from his tone of voice that this promise meant a great deal to him. Here's how he described it in his own words:

"I recall very vividly the day my first son was born. For whatever reason that day I felt compelled … I felt compelled to get into a shower and I scrubbed myself from head to toe. And my belief was that this was the day I was being given a gift from God. And for the nine months preceding this day, God had taken care of my unborn son … and when my son was born I made a promise to God: 'Thank you so much for taking care of my child up until now. And now I promise to take beautiful care of the child you've given me the responsibility to raise in the best way that I know how.'

"And that was a very, very clear promise that I made when both of my children were born. And really I believe that it was a partnership created not only between me and my boys but between me and God. And that I would do anything and everything to fulfill that promise. This was 13-15 years ago … and as soon as I was asked 'When have I made a promise' and I remember having the dialogue in my heart and in my mind with God … making that promise. And when this opportunity came to share this story with you … I thought that's one that I think would be at least worthwhile expressing the seriousness to me of that promise and the relationship that I have with my boys today as a result of fulfilling that promise."

Later in the interview, John elaborated a little more on the promise he made to God and how much it meant to him. He makes clear that this promise was emotionally powerful to him.

"On this particular day, I felt compelled to scrub myself ... from head to toe, as if my child was being handed over to me from God's hands to my hands. That was a feeling that I'll never forget and a promise that I'll never forget. And even as I think about it I'm getting a little choked up. It's like you said: I made a promise. And I made a promise to God! You can't go back on it. That's a promise you don't want to go back on."

Adherents of the Catholic faith often direct their prayers to Catholic saints, asking for some sort of blessing and promising to give something in return. A work colleague told me about one such prayer and promise made by her mother made when my colleague, at the time a young student, prayed to Saint Christopher, the patron saint of travelers and of children, to return her daughter safely to her after her studies abroad. In return, my colleague's mother promised that while her daughter was away, she would give up drinking coffee. She loved to drink coffee, so giving it up was a real sacrifice that she promised to make out of concern for her daughter's safety. The mother kept her word, and her daughter returned safely home after spending a year in Europe.

This kind of promise absolutely requires that you live up to your end of the bargain. After all, God and other higher powers carry such attributes as being all-seeing and all-knowing. So, it is impossible to cheat. God, like Santa Claus, knows whether you've been naughty or nice.

Her mother, my colleague explained, couldn't sneak a sip of coffee without Saint Christopher and God knowing it, which would very well endanger the welfare of her daughter. This built-in fail-safe system made for a very powerful promise indeed.

WHAT'S YOUR PROMISE?

Danny Thomas' Promise to Saint Jude

Danny Thomas was a talented and successful television actor and producer in the 1950s and 1960s, an exciting, groundbreaking era in the history of television. But achieving success didn't come easily for him. Early in his career, while supporting a growing family, he struggled to get gigs in radio and as a nightclub comedian.

As his daughter, Marlo Thomas, an actress and activist, described it: "Earlier in his life when times were tough, [my father] reached a turning point as a struggling actor and a father-to-be; Mom was actually pregnant with me at that time. He sought guidance in prayer and called upon Saint Jude, the patron saint of hopeless causes. My father made a promise, saying that if Saint Jude would show him his way in life, he would erect a shrine in his honor."

Soon after, his career took off with roles in network radio, film and the long running network television show, "Make Room for Daddy," later known as "The Danny Thomas Show." He became a producer of television hits like "The Dick Van Dyke Show" and "The Mod Squad."

With his success, Thomas stayed true to his promise: In 1962, he founded St. Jude Children's Research Hospital in Memphis, Tennessee, [https://www.stjude.org] to treat children suffering from catastrophic illnesses. To this day, children from all over the world are accepted for treatment at the hospital, regardless of their family's ability to pay. Any costs that health insurance doesn't cover, and the entire costs of families who don't have insurance, are covered. Thomas made sure this would be the case by creating a funding organization that also honors his Lebanese and Syrian descent. The American Lebanese Syrian Associated Charities raises $350 million a year.

Danny passed away in 1991, but the legacy of his promise is carried on today by Marlo, who serves as the National Outreach Director for the hospital, which has become one of the world's premier centers for pediatric cancer treatment and research. She hosts the annual fundraiser, the St. Jude Hollywood Gala, as well as "Time to Live," an hour-long television special that documents the impact of the hospital's lifesaving work. In addition, the hospital receives all proceeds from her bestselling, inspirational book, "The Right Words at the Right Time."

WHAT'S YOUR PROMISE?

A Promise to Love by Princess Merrilee

(https://merrileeofsolana.com)

[In her own words]

Circa 2009, on the cusp of an impending life change, I turned to my Bible. Reading the words I had read so many times before, hit me a little different on that night I sat in my chair.

Verse after verse seemed to repeat the same message loud and clear. The way is to love. All that was asked of me in exchange for an eternal promise was love.

Clearly love wasn't so simple because many people love and many people suffer without experiencing a promise.

My heart was broken, I had been disappointed, betrayed, and abused, but I also thought I was loved, and I was loving. The Bible says, God is love. If God is love, the reverse must also be true. If love is God, did I know God? Considering others, did they know God? I wanted to know God and I wanted to experience the promise.

Love, it turns out, is not so easy. Loving correctly meant I was not to be the cause of any suffering. I was to stop the pain by Just Being Love. Nothing Else. Being One with God, knowing love, and experiencing the promise became my single and narrow focus. The following years became moment to moment tests of my commitment. It didn't take long to realize I had made a promise that others clearly had not. While others continued to be the cause of pain, I stood my ground, held my tongue, and learned how to respond, trying my best not to be the cause of pain.

Not causing pain would require a lot of restraint. I couldn't defend myself when others made assumptions, I had to stop making accusations and instead learn to ask questions.

I stopped making excuses and learned to accept responsibility without defense. I had to learn to let others make their own mistakes without imposing my opinion. The lessons cut deep into my ego, hurt my self-esteem, and challenged my ability to let others have their opinion of me without correcting the record.

I also learned to consider what I wanted to say before saying it, then consider their response based on what I said to eliminate any possibility of defense, excuses, or blame. To be love, my goal was to diffuse the ego and invoke a loving response.

My promise to Just Be Love is absolutely attainable. I can tell you with certainty that life is very different when you see a favorable reflection in people and God's favor is all around you.

That mirror is who I AM. I am Love. One with God. The promise delivered.

[Author's Note: Princess Merrilee of Solana; Mentor, Speaker, Award Winning author- THE GAME, Winning by Virtue One Move at a Time, Protagonist, "Deals Danger Destiny" memoir series by John LaCasse and Advocate for Love. https://merrileeofsolana.com]

Sometimes a promise doesn't fall neatly into just one category. Here's an example of a promise that Laura Templeton made to both God and to herself.

WHAT'S YOUR PROMISE?

Laura Templeton's Promise to Herself and to God

[In her own words]

Years ago, during a very dark and lonely time, I made a promise – to myself and to God – that I would never give up on the work He set before me. At the time, I had no idea how much that promise would shape my life. I simply knew that my faith was my foundation, and that whatever path lay ahead, I would walk it with unwavering commitment.

That promise has carried me through many seasons – each one different yet deeply connected by the thread of God's purpose. From pursuing my education and stepping into a successful executive career, to building a marriage that has lasted 37 years, to raising and homeschooling two incredible children, to launching my own business and stepping fully into entrepreneurship, the work has evolved. But through every shift, every challenge, and every unexpected turn, one thing has remained constant: my commitment to start every day in His presence and to wait on Him.

There have been times when I faltered, times when I doubted, and times when I wanted to give up because the burden felt too heavy or the way forward seemed unclear. But that promise – that sacred commitment – has been my anchor. It has reminded me that my work is not about worldly success or recognition, but about obedience, impact, and faithfulness.

That promise has changed me. It has shaped my character, deepened my resilience, and refined my purpose. It has taught me that success is not measured in titles or achievements but in the lives touched, the love given, and the faith sustained through trials. It has also changed the lives of those around me – my family, friends, clients, and those I've been called to serve. When we choose to stand firm in our calling, even when it's hard and we don't see the full picture, we inspire others to do the same.

This journey of faith and perseverance has made me a better wife, mother, mentor, and leader. It has allowed me to speak into the lives of others with wisdom gained from experience, show up with compassion, and help others embrace their own God-given calling with confidence.

I don't know what the future holds, but I do know this: my promise still stands. As long as I have breath, I will continue to trust, serve, and walk the path He has set before me – one faithful step at a time.

[Author's Note: Laura Templeton is a Speaker, Author, Brand Communication Strategist, and Founder of 30 Second Success. https://30secondsuccess.com/]

If you've made a promise to God or another higher power, I encourage you to do the following exercise to explore that promise more fully. Before you start, please read through the steps to get a feel for the entire process. And use your Promise Journal to make notes about your experience when you finish.

INWARD BOUND

Explore a Promise Made to God or a Higher Power

Sit or lie down in a comfortable, quiet place where you won't be disturbed for about 30 minutes. Close your eyes. Take three to five deep, relaxing breaths, in and out slowly.

Recall a promise you made to God or a higher power. It could be a small promise that you made and kept without much effort, or it could be a big, ambitious promise that led to dramatic, life-changing results. Or it could be something in between. (Alternatively, you could think about a promise you are considering making to God and adapt this exercise accordingly.)

Think back to what prompted your promise. What was going on in your life and how did you feel about it? Why did you make the promise to God in the first place?

Now try to recall the process of making your promise:

- Did you spend some time thinking about it, or did your promise spring into your mind suddenly and maybe even fully formed?
- What was the wording of your promise? Did you use the words "I promise?" Did you state your promise directly to the other person? Did you write it down? Perhaps you did both.

Revisit the feelings you experienced when you made your promise. Perhaps you were full of happy anticipation? Maybe you felt love for God, and from God.

Finally, consider how your promise turned out:

- Did you keep your promise? What impact has this had in your life and in the lives of others? And how do you feel about keeping your promise?
- Maybe you didn't keep your promise. Are you still working on it? Think about what prevented you from keeping your promise. Don't beat yourself up over this; simply gather information that could help you in the future.

As you conclude this exercise, slowly return your awareness to the room you're in and open your eyes. Make notes in your Promise Journal to "lock in" your insights from this exercise. You might also want to start thinking about a new promise you'd like to make to God or a higher power. Think about the details of the promise and why you want to make it.

A FEW THOUGHTS ABOUT PROMISES *FROM* GOD

For many people, the word "promise" may have religious connotations attached to it, especially regarding the idea that God makes promises to us. Without going into a long discussion about the religious aspects of promises (it would take an entire book to begin to do justice to that topic), I will comment here that the religious power of the word "promise" almost certainly contributes to the unique power of this word in our lives and in society more generally.

I begin by sharing an anonymous quote that I find particularly appealing and poetic:

"No pillow so soft as God's promise."

The Bible records many promises made by God, promises that can resonate in very personal and powerful ways among those of the Jewish and Christian faiths. Among these are:

- **Joshua 23:14, NIV:** "You know with all your heart and soul that not one of all the good promises the Lord your God gave you has failed. Every promise has been fulfilled; not one has failed."
- **2 Peter 1:4, NLT:** "And because of his glory and excellence, he has given us great and precious promises. These are the promises that enable you to share his divine nature and escape the world's corruption caused by human desires."

- **Genesis 24:7, NCV:** "Abraham said, 'The Lord brought me from the land of my relatives to this land, and he has solemnly promised me that would give this land to my descendants.'"
- **II Corinthians 1:19-20, NKJV:** "For the Son of God, Jesus Christ, who was preached among you by us – by me, Silvanus, and Timothy – was not Yes and No, but in Him was Yes. For all the promises of God in Him are Yes, and in Him Amen, to the glory of God through us."
- **Luke 1:37, NIV:** "Nothing is impossible with respect to any of God's promises."
- **I John 2:25, NKJV:** "And this is the promise that He has promised us – eternal life."
- **Psalm 18:30, NLT:** "God's way is perfect. All the LORD's promises prove true. He is a shield for all who look to him for protection."
- **Hebrews 6:12, NLT:** "Then you will not become spiritually dull and indifferent. Instead, you will follow the example of those who are going to inherit God's promises because of their faith and endurance."
- **Hebrews 11:17, ASV:** "By faith Abraham, being tried, offered up Isaac: yea, he that had gladly received the promises was offering up his only begotten son."

A FEW FINAL REFLECTIONS ABOUT THE "WHO-TO'S" OF PROMISES

As this chapter draws to a close, I offer a point of clarification: The three "who-to's" of promise-making aren't necessarily mutually exclusive. Most promises do tend to find their way into the category that seems to have just the right "fit" for it, but there is no requirement that any given promise must fall into one and only one of these categories. Some promises we make to ourselves, for example, could also be made to someone we care about or to a higher power.

In fact, it could be argued that a promise made to two or even all three categories is more powerful than a promise made in only one. Covering all three bases by making every promise to yourself, *and* someone you care about, *and* a higher power can be a highly effective strategy for increasing your chances of following through.

Also, without getting too metaphysical about it, let me posit that all three "Who-to" categories just might boil down to the same thing. In the final analysis, we always make promises to someone we care about – be that someone ourselves, another person, or a higher power. And this could be what gives promises their special, heart-centered, even magical powers.

Think about it. Promises that we make to ourselves are especially powerful, because we care about ourselves and our integrity. It comes down to the relationship you have with yourself and your own conscience. You must look at yourself in the mirror. If you get into the habit of making and keeping promises, you're going to be much more comfortable with the person you see in the mirror staring back at you. If that's not the case, then your promise to yourself would have very little meaning.

When all is said and done, when it comes to promises you make to yourself what matters most is your level of personal integrity. If you make a promise to yourself, the onus of following through is completely on you. You will either fulfill your promise or not depending on how much personal integrity you possess and your sense of self-worth.

A promise made to a loved one or dear friend is obviously made to someone we care about. If you choose to make a promise to another person, it's important to choose wisely. Make a promise to someone whose opinion matters to you. Someone you look up to. Someone to whom you want to bring feelings of joy and pride by keeping your word, and who you know would be disappointed in you if your break your promise.

If you choose to make a promise to God or some other deity or higher power, it must be because you care about God and have deep faith. And this faith will serve as an added reinforcement, to buttress the power of a promise with your belief in a higher power. As John Assaraf said, "I made a promise to God! You can't go back on it. That's a promise you don't want to go back on." Now that's affirming belief and faith in God!

In the end, the promises you make and your ability to honor your promises all comes down to you. You must master the first habit of SUCCESS, "Shoulder Responsibility," that I discuss in detail in Chapter 6. To take 100% responsibility for your life – as Jack Canfield discusses extensively in *The Success Principles* – you must make a habit of keeping the promises you make to yourself, to others, and to a higher power. No ifs, ands, or buts.

Now we begin the journey, aided by the four booster rockets of the four-part promise mantra, to achieving your goals, changing your life and, ultimately, transforming the world. So please turn the page to Chapter 4: Make a Promise, where you'll learn about turning goals into promises and discover the seven tips for making and keeping powerful promises. You're now on the edge of the New Frontier in personal change and achievement. You're on the verge of harnessing your *PromisePower* and putting it to work for you as you begin to change your life and transform the world, one promise at a time.

"Go for it now. The future is promised to no one."
– Wayne Dyer

CHAPTER 4

Make a Promise: The G.P.S. Success Formula

From Goals to Promises = Success

7 TIPS FOR MAKING AND KEEPING PROMISES

This is the chapter where the rubber meets the road. Where you put into action what you have learned in the previous chapters. Where you "go for it," as Wayne Dyer put it.

You've read about what can be achieved by harnessing the power of a promise. About Believing More, Achieving More and Receiving More. About the anatomy of promises made to yourself, to someone you care, and to God or deity or higher power. I hope you've also been inspired by the stories of people who have made and kept some quite extraordinary promises.

Now it's time to take the Promise Challenge, perhaps starting by turning a vague wish or a "someday" dream into a concrete promise. Maybe you're already quite clear about goals you'd like to achieve. Now, using the G.P.S. Success Formula, you'll turn your goals into promises that keep you on track and moving forward. You'll also learn about seven simple and very effective tools for making and keeping promises.

THE PROMISE MANTRA: FOUR BOOSTER ROCKETS FOR POWERFUL PROMISES

A word here about structure. This chapter is the first of four devoted to, and named for, the four parts of my Promise Mantra capturing the immense power of a promise:

Make a Promise
Keep Your Word
Change Your Life
Transform the World

Each part of this four-part mantra is like a booster rocket, with each stage adding extra propulsion toward keeping your promises and reaching your destination. In this chapter, we'll look at both the broad strokes and finer points of making a promise. Chapter 5: Keep Your Word, focuses on following through on your promises. In Chapter 6, we'll explore how promises can Change Your Life, concluding with Chapter 7: Transform the World.

So, let's get going! We begin our journey with a powerful visualization exercise. In this one, you will explore taking the Promise Challenge with a promise you're thinking about making. The self-awareness this exercise can provide will guide you in creating a promise-centered life.

I suggest you first read through the entire exercise for an overall sense of the process. You'll want to pull out your Promise Journal to make notes on insights, feelings and anything else that comes up for you during this exercise. If you prefer, you can keep notes on your smartphone or another digital device, but there's something about writing them down on paper that helps keeps you more closely connected with your inner process.

INWARD BOUND

Taking the Promise Challenge

Sit or lie down in a comfortable, quiet place where you won't be disturbed for about 30 minutes. Close your eyes. Take three to five deep, relaxing breaths, in and out slowly.

Think about a promise you'd like to make. It could be a promise to yourself, to someone you care about or to a higher power. It could be something small that pops into your mind as you do this exercise, or it could be an important goal you've had for quite some time but haven't steadfastly pursued.

Now imagine yourself making your promise. Notice: Who are you making this promise to? Yourself? Someone else? God or a higher power? And what words do you use in making your promise?

Pay attention to how you feel while you make your promise. Maybe you're happy or excited. But maybe what you're feeling is something else – not feeling very confident, perhaps, maybe even feeling some fear or anxiety. If negative feelings like these come up, try redirecting the promise to yourself or someone else and see how you feel now.

Envision yourself following through on your promise and observe:

- What are some of the first steps you take to follow through? What changes in your life do you make?
- How are your life and the lives of others changed by keeping this promise?
- How does it feel to keep your promise?

As you conclude this exercise, slowly return your awareness to the room you're in and open your eyes. Chances are good that you had some fresh and perhaps even surprising insights. Make notes about your feelings and insights in your Promise Journal to "lock in" their lessons and have them available for future reference.

Maybe you feel ready to take the Promise Challenge right now with a promise you're raring to make, and that's great! I suggest that first you jump ahead in this chapter to the 7 Tips for Making and Keeping a Promise.

THE G.P.S. SUCCESS FORMULA: FROM GOALS TO PROMISES = SUCCESS

Got goals? We all do. At least a few. At this very moment, you can probably name a half-dozen goals right off the top of your head, from "finish reading this book" to taking a vacation in some little corner of paradise. It's good to have lots of goals because goals keep you energized and inspired, always thinking of ways to reach them. They keep you visualizing about a positive future. But goals can also be frustrating if you find yourself not reaching them. Goals unrealized can weigh you down with regrets and disempower you.

Often, we have vague wishes instead of concrete goals. It's okay to have dreams, to know in general terms some of the things we would like to do, see and accomplish in our lives. But having vague ideas about the future is seldom sufficient. Don't settle for a bunch of "Someday I'll" daydreams that never materialize. Success in life depends on turning wishes, dreams and goals into reality. The old saying is true: A goal is a dream with a deadline.

Generally speaking, we are goal-driven creatures whose very survival depends on having, expressing, acting upon and fulfilling various goals. As infants we all had the goal of relieving an uncomfortable, empty feeling in our stomachs. We wanted to be fed and so we'd let loose with a loud wail that let our parents or other grownups know we needed to be fed. Or have our diapers changed. Or that we wanted to be held and comforted.

Early in life our goals and the things we did to reach them were innate, instinctive, built in. As we matured, becoming more conscious about our lives and the things we want to do and achieve, we started to become more aware of making choices. As we transition from childhood to adulthood, we realize that we have the power to make decisions and take steps toward our goals – sometimes long-term goals, big goals about our life's purpose. Once we start to realize that we have the power to make decisions and set goals, it becomes our responsibility to figure out the best methods for turning goals into reality.

A PROMISE IS LIKE A GOAL ON STEROIDS

At different points in this book, Jack Canfield, John Assaraf, Bill Bartmann and others offer their thoughts about the difference between a goal and a promise. I won't belabor that discussion at this stage. Suffice it to say here that goals and promises bear similarities. But there is a difference.

Napoleon Hill is credited with coining the phrase "A goal is a dream with a deadline." That's a very succinct way of putting it.

With that in mind, I will share a thought that has recently occurred to me. Perhaps we should think of a promise as a goal with a conscience. Or perhaps as a goal with a conscience and a heart.

I have suggested several times in this book that a promise is like a goal on steroids. This entire book springs from my fundamental belief that a promise is a uniquely powerful way to reach goals and to do what we say we want to do. That's the promise premise in brief. Infants don't have to think about their goals or figure out ways to reach them. As adults, it's on us to make something of our lives and, hopefully, make the world a better place.

It's great to have the power of choice, but that power involves taking responsibility for our lives. Life becomes more complicated. The answers aren't built in. And too often, even if we know what we want to achieve and we know what we're supposed to do to get there, we don't always follow through or take consistent action. And a great idea or a specific goal often withers on the vine of procrastination, inaction, and wishful thinking. Like my failed Comedy TV idea that I shared with you earlier, much to my chagrin. I blew it because I didn't pursue it. I dropped the ball. I don't want you to drop the ball on great ideas and important goals in your life.

This chapter is about taking an indispensable first step toward taking charge of our lives. Deciding to use the most effective tools we have available for making and reaching goals. This is where turning goals into promises can make all the difference, because most people are loath to break their promises. We know instinctively that it's wrong. Most people will bend over backwards to avoid breaking a promise. This is not usually the case, certainly not to the same degree, when it comes to setting and keeping goals.

As mentioned earlier, Napoleon Hill of *Think and Grow Rich* fame recognized the power of making a promise as part of the first step in his five-step self-confidence formula for achievement. Here's how Hill describes what readers should say to themselves:

"Step One: I know that I have the ability to achieve the object of my definite purpose in life; therefore, I demand of myself persistent, continuous action toward its attainment, and I here and now ***PROMISE*** *to render such action." (My emphasis.)*

Promises can jack up the power of the goals many of us set for ourselves in our pursuit of self-improvement. That's why I coined the concept of Personal Empowerment Promises. These are promises that relate to being, doing and having more in our lives. Moving beyond our status quo to higher levels of achievement and fulfillment. Many of us – millions of us – read self-help books, watch videos or attend workshops on topics as wide-ranging as improving your health, finding your soul mate, handling finances, being a better parent, building a money-making business and expanding your consciousness. At some point most, if not all, of these programs will bring up the subject of setting goals. As well they should, since goal setting is an excellent and even essential tool for setting out what we really want to be, do and have.

In my forthcoming book, *Harness Your HabitForce*, I refer to this kind of goal setting as "Setting Your Course." Mapping out the direction you plan to take in some specific area of your life – such as setting a career goal, deciding to write a book, getting involved in an organization that addresses a cause that's important to you.

For Jack Canfield, goal setting is a foundational constant throughout his books, videos, website, workshops and coaching programs. In "Unleash the Power of Goal-Setting," Principle #7 in his bestselling book, *The Success Principles*, Jack recommends writing down at least 101 goals you want to achieve in your life.

"Setting goals is critically important for achievement and success in life, however you define success," he notes, adding examples of goals from his own list that he has already happily accomplished, including traveling to Africa, learning to ski, and writing a children's book. Jack's success in accomplishing his goals speaks to his formidable focus and commitment.

For many of us, unfortunately, the goals we list with great excitement and fanfare don't take long to morph into just another to-do list, more burden than benefit.

This is where turning goals into promises, selectively, can make a big difference. As John Assaraf told me during his "What's Your Promise?" interview:

"There is something uniquely powerful about making a promise that goes beyond traditional goal setting. Setting a promise takes it to a whole new dimension."

SUPERCHARGE YOUR PERSONAL EMPOWERMENT EFFORTS

One major appeal of using *PromisePower* as a personal empowerment strategy is that it can be incorporated into many existing systems and programs already being championed by other writers and success coaches. The Make-a-Promise approach fits neatly into other success systems. It does not conflict with or undermine what other authors and coaches already teach. In fact, it augments what other leading authorities already espouse. Any program or activity that requires setting goals and a long-term commitment for achievement is an ideal candidate for making use of my G.P.S. Success Formula – From Goals to Promises = Success. This is a value-added approach.

The unique power of making a promise derives from the fact that a promise is heart centered. A promise comes from the heart and is backed by a deep emotional commitment. Because your emotions are engaged, a promise means you have some real skin in the game.

Setting goals, stating intentions, making resolutions are all well and good, but these tend to be more cerebral, brain-centered in nature. Not exclusively, of course, but predominantly.

Clearly stated, my premise about a promise is this: A promise is more powerful because it comes from the heart and is charged with emotional commitment.

This was true of the promise I made to my mother. It was true of the promises to God described by both John Assaraf and Jack Canfield (see below). It's true of the promise Tony Robbins made when he was 11 years old and the promise Bill Clinton made to his daughter, Chelsea. Brendon Burchard made a promise to God that came from the heart. Oprah Winfry's promise to Nelson Mandela was backed by strong emotion. The heart connection of a promise makes all the difference.

As Emmy Award-winning TV host Todd Newton said in his "What's Your Promise?" interview, making a promise sends a powerful message about how strongly you care about a particular goal or objective. A promise says, in Newton's words, "This is important enough to me that I'm going to promise to do it. I'm taking this very seriously and I'm deeply committed to the outcome."

The same thing simply cannot be said about a traditional goal or objective. In this book and related programs, I encourage people to take the Promise Challenge by turning important goals into heartfelt promises. Why? Because a promise significantly increases the likelihood that you will follow through, that you will do what you say you're going to do. There are no guarantees, of course. But a promise sharply enhances your chances of making good on your commitment.

Making a promise is your secret superpower in your personal-change arsenal. If you want to make a change or achieve anything in your life, start by making a promise – a personal empowerment promise. Making a promise that you're going to do something locks you in emotionally and makes it clear both to you and anybody else involved that failure is not an option. I'll say it again: You can *change* a goal, but you can only *break* a promise. And most people are loath to break their promises.

You see, once you make a promise, a transformation takes place. I sometimes think of a promise as the connective tissue between a dream or a goal or objective and the action required to achieve it. The promise connects you to the action. It's almost as if the promise supplies the energy and motivation you need to take continuous action toward achieving the promise.

When you make a promise, you wake up every day knowing that you've made that promise and all sorts of forces – your conscience, your accountability to yourself and others, your integrity, your emotions – come into play. That's how you keep action going. Because of the promise.

It's a motivator. It's one of the reasons that people who make promises tend to achieve quite a bit in life. They stay in action because they've made a promise.

Staying the course with goals, on the other hand, can get sketchy. Every one of us has fallen short of reaching one goal or another. I certainly have. Sometimes I started off strong but then I lost steam over time or tripped myself up by changing the goal along the way – maybe even several times along the way. Other times I fizzled out because my heart just wasn't in it and I started thinking it wasn't such a big deal. After all, it was "just a goal," just one of many goals.

Unlike goals or intentions, a promise poses a challenge. We know about the concept of a reality check. Well … Making a promise requires what I call an "integrity check." When you make a promise, your integrity is on the line. My advice: Don't make a promise until you've done an honest, heartfelt integrity check.

7 TIPS FOR MAKING AND KEEPING PROMISES

Here's a handy list of seven tips so you have them conveniently in one place. I suggest that you write these tips down in your Promise Journal and refer to them frequently.

7 TIPS FOR MAKING AND KEEPING PROMISES

1. Start Small
2. Be Selective
3. Be Specific
4. Commit Emotionally
5. Write It

6. Share It
7. Follow Through

Note that this list is intentionally spare. Just two words for each tip, making them easy to remember. These are not arranged as steps to take in sequence, although it goes without saying that the seventh and final tip – Follow Through – must always come after the other six. Also, note that many of these seven tips overlap somewhat. There is not a clear borderline between them. A selective promise is often a specific promise and one that you commit to emotionally. So, these, although not mutually exclusive, are important and sufficiently distinct to warrant a separate discussion with a few promise stories to illustrate each of them in turn.

Now, let's consider these tips one at a time.

TIP 1: START SMALL

I encourage you to start with one or two small promises that are relatively easy to accomplish. Why? Because it's important to get into the habit of keeping promises. This should become second nature. And for that to happen you should build up your achievement muscles by doing what you say you're going to do right from the start.

Yes, it's a good idea to take on big, important goals, to turn those into promises that will make a very big difference in your life and the lives of those around you. But I don't think it's a good idea to start out with promises that are too ambitious because the idea here is to gain confidence in your ability to make a promise and keep it. So, starting small is a good, realistic step in the right direction. It's a confidence-building measure.

"A journey of a thousand miles begins with a single step."
- Lao Tzu

This same approach works well with promises: Break your big promises into small, manageable promises.

Here are some suggestions for small, easy-to-achieve promises that you could make today.

- I promise to get up at 6:00 a.m. on workdays.
- I promise to make my bed every morning.
- I promise to say "I love you" every day to someone special.
- I promise to get to work on time.
- I promise to floss my teeth every night.

Use your imagination and quickly come up with several promises along these lines. Think about small promises you could make that could add up to accomplishing something you've been meaning to do for a long time but haven't quite gotten around to.

But don't make too many promises at once. Don't set yourself up for failure. Try just one or two easy-to-accomplish goals for the first month and notice what happens. Even if you choose just a couple of simple promises, be sure to follow the other tips below. No matter how small the promise is, these tips will help you keep your word, discussed in greater detail in the next chapter.

You could identify a slightly more ambitious goal to turn into a promise. Here again, it's best to keep the promise focused on small increments. Don't bite off too much because if you make a promise and fall short, you will undermine your promise-keeping confidence. It's very important not to do that. Try baby steps first and then start promising to take on bigger goals.

For example, let's say you'd like to learn a foreign language. Don't promise to become fluent in six months or even a year. Make a promise to study the language for 30 minutes or an hour every day. Something you can manage easily. Or let's say you want to read more of the greatest books ever written. Don't promise to read 50 books this year. Instead, make a promise to read one book each month.

Maybe you'd like to lose some weight. Get started by promising to reach a couple of realistic goals. You might want to lose a total of 20 pounds (or even more). But I'd like to see you promise to lose 5 pounds over the next month and do a little more exercise and cut back on your calories. Or promise to lose two pounds a week for the next month. That's a very achievable goal. Backed by the power of a promise, you'll do it! Record your progress frequently in your Promise Journal. Pretty soon you'll see a few pounds vanish and you'll feel great. You kept your promise! And you should celebrate that victory.

A few small victories like that will help to strengthen your promise-keeping muscles. Now you'll be ready to renew the promise for the following month or even ratchet up the promise to lose a little more weight. Build on your successes.

By contrast, let's say you promised to lose 20 pounds in a month. That's a very ambitious goal, one that you're unlikely to achieve. So, what happens when you fall short of that goal? You've broken your promise and feel like a failure. Undermining your confidence is not what this process is about. It's about doing the opposite: Empowering you, building up your self-confidence and feelings of self-worth.

Please note that you should always consult with your doctor if you're contemplating a major weight loss program.

As part of a promise to lose weight and become more physically fit, you could consider making smaller promises such as "Do five or 10 pushups every day for a month." Or "Walk 15 minutes every day." Make sure you choose realistic, doable goals. Don't begin with a promise that's too much of a stretch. Start small to establish the habit of making and keeping promises.

Progress toward any goal or any promise is made one step at a time – even one day, one minute or one hour at a time. If you've ever wondered how Leo Tolstoy wrote the epic novel, "War and Peace," the answer is one word at a time – all 587,287 of them! The same approach would apply to learning a new language. We learn languages one word at a time too.

Mark Twain said, "The secret of getting started is breaking your complex overwhelming tasks into small manageable tasks and starting on the first one." When pursuing a promise, even a very big promise, each step toward fulfilling it is a small step. Thinking in terms of small steps helps you keep perspective. It helps you avoid feeling overwhelmed by a very big, ambitious goal that could take years to attain. Thinking small steps will help to motivate you to continue the journey. Every step you take, however small, is leading toward your goal.

Sonia's "Clean-Living" Promise

During a workshop I was giving about my book *Habit-Force!*, I noticed a woman in the front row whose eyes seemed to light up when I mentioned the promise made to my mother that motivated me to finish that book and led to all sorts of other positive changes in my life. The woman,

I'll call her "Sonia" – hurried up to me at the next break and very excitedly told me about a small promise that she made to herself when she was 20 years old that led to more small promises and big benefits in her life.

"I promised myself that I would wash my dirty dishes every day," Sonia began. "I know that might sound ridiculous to most people, but for me promising to wash my dishes was a big deal."

Sonia had been living on her own for a year, working at an office job that paid her just enough to rent a tiny one-room apartment and buy groceries. "I had stuff spread all over the floor and bed, my one piece of furniture. Clothes, newspapers, mail, nail polish, earrings – you name it. Along one wall there was a little kitchenette with a sink where I left dirty dishes soaking until finally I'd run out of clean dishes and have to wash the dirty ones. It was all pretty disgusting."

Then one day she found herself unhappily slogging through a week's worth of dirty dishes, pouring dishwashing soap over them in the sink. Suddenly she noticed the name on the dish soap bottle – "Dawn" – and a split-second later it "dawned" on her that she needed to clean up the dirty dishes and messy apartment.

"It was at that moment," she explained, "standing at the sink in my little kitchenette, that I promised myself to wash my dirty dishes every day. I kept that promise and, by the way, I still keep it today."

The satisfaction Sonia felt in keeping that promise led to other, similar promises to hang up her clothes, throw away old newspapers, clear away countertops and stow things in cabinets. Before long, the mess in Sonia's apartment disappeared, never to return, because of that one simple promise to herself.

Sonia added: "I realized – again, it 'dawned' on me – that the lessons of orderliness and cleanliness that I never learned as a child were lessons I could teach myself as an adult."

Over the ensuing 20 years, Sonia has continued to learn new ways of being and has continued to make new promises that extend into everything from cultivating healthy, loving relationships to managing her portfolio of lucrative financial investments.

"I call it my 'clean-living life,'" Sonia said, "that started with a sink full of dirty dishes."

For the purposes of this book, I would call it a "promise-powered life," one that can serve as a lesson and inspiration to us all. Sonia started small, built up her promise-keeping muscles, and eventually moved on to make other life-changing promises.

"Never promise more than you can perform."
- Publilius Syrus, 1st Century B.C.

You probably have some big goals, and you might be tempted to turn them into promises. I just want to caution you again not to bite off more than you can chew. Take it slow to begin with. It's better to start with more manageable promises and work your way up to bigger goals after you've kept your word several times.

TIP 2: BE SELECTIVE

As you start your journey along this promising path, I suggest that you pick just one or two important goals and turn them into heartfelt promises. Frankly, not all goals are created equal, and not all goals require the firepower of a promise. I suggest that you select a couple of important goals and turn them into heartfelt promises.

But don't go overboard with too many promises, or you'll lose track and get distracted and very likely frustrated. Making and keeping a couple of promises to start with will do wonders in building your confidence so you'll feel empowered to take on a few more promises in the future.

In this book and in my PEPTalks programs, I issue what I refer to as the Promise Challenge: Of all the goals in your life, of all your hopes and dreams, all the items on your wish list and bucket list, which ones are important enough to you that you're willing to put your integrity on the line to achieve?

Dr. Richard Davidson, a neuroscientist and founder of the Center for Investigating Healthy Minds at the University of Wisconsin-Madison, was selective when he made a promise to his friend and confidante the Dalai Lama that he would "put compassion on the scientific map." Davidson is now studying whether meditation can promote compassion and kindness. Davidson had met the Dalai Lama and was a big admirer of his. Making a promise to him regarding the scientific study of compassion was a significant step for Davidson. He was extremely thoughtful and selective in making this promise.

Another example of being selective is the promise made by Christopher Gardner when he was still a child. Gardner is the author of "In Pursuit of Happyness," which was also made into a movie starring Will Smith. Here's how he described the promise he made to himself:

"I made a promise to myself as a little boy that became a commitment I kept as a man that when I had children, they would know their father. I would break the cycle of children who didn't know who their fathers were. It is still the most important thing I've ever done in my life."

Al Roker, popular anchor and weatherman on the "Today Show," famously made a promise to his dying father that he would deal with a longstanding weight problem. At the time, going on two decades ago, Al was tipping the scales at about 340 pounds.

His promise was prompted by a conversation with his father.

"One morning," Al recalled, "he said to me: 'Look. You've got to promise me that you're going to lose weight. We both know I'm not going to be here to help you with my grandchildren. So, you've got to promise me."

Al made that promise to his father and, true to his word, kept it, despite encountering a few hurdles along the way. With the help of gastric bypass surgery, he quickly shed 140 pounds and dropped 20 suit sizes. But soon after, he began to regain some of that weight because gastric bypass surgery, which essentially reduces the caloric intake of food by reducing the size of the stomach and bypassing the small intestine, didn't require him to change his eating habits. One of those habits was to eat when he felt stressed. When his mother was hospitalized a few years after his initial weight loss, for example, he turned to food for solace and quickly gained 40 pounds.

"I went back … and I hated it," he recalled in an interview with "Today Show" medical correspondent Nancy Snyderman. Finally, he was able to "put on the brakes," as he described it, and bring his weight down through a combination of diet and exercise. "I'm thrilled about where I am," Al said. "Life is terrific; I wouldn't trade it for a moment."

That's the power of making a promise. I'm sure Al, along with countless millions of other people, set many goals and made several unsuccessful New Year's Resolutions centered on his desire to lose weight. He had known for years about his weight problem. But it took that heartfelt promise to his father for Al to find the determination and fortitude to make it happen.

Clearly, Al was selective. He didn't make a bunch of promises. He made this one big promise to his dying father, which infused the promise with enormous emotional power. Please note that this promise illustrates how these seven tips often overlap. They're not mutually exclusive. A selective promise (Tip 2: Be Selective) can also be one that is packed with emotional intensity (Tip 4: Commit Emotionally).

We must make choices about the promises we make. We need to set priorities. A selective, well-chosen promise can define your life's work, your passion and your mission in life. One well-chosen promise can change the entire trajectory of your life in ways that you don't even imagine at the time. A single promise can lead you to discover your true passions and define your life's work. That's what Roslyn Franken experienced when her initial promise to lose weight turned into a lifetime mission to help others take great care of themselves in every respect.

So, pick an important goal and set it into motion by enlisting the heartfelt commitment of those two magic words: "I promise."

TIP 3: BE SPECIFIC

Specificity generates electricity! You can't get energized by, or committed to, vague generalities. Trying to fulfill vague promises is like trying to hit a moving target – an exercise in frustration.

An effective promise is a specific promise. Instead of making a vague promise to "lose weight," determine specifically what weight you want to see register on your scale, and by what specific date.

Instead of making a promise to "get regular exercise," promise to do a specific number of push-ups or sit-ups (or both!). Promise to walk a specific distance or for a specific period of time. Be specific about what days of the week you'll exercise and set "dates" with yourself in advance on your calendar.

Let's say you want to learn French. Making a promise that "I'm going to learn French" certainly leans in the right direction, but wording like that probably isn't going to hack it in the long run. You need to get your promise down to specifics. For starters, what specifically do you mean when you say you're going to "learn French?" Do you want to learn just enough of the language to be able to order from a menu in French from a fancy French restaurant in Paris? Or is it your intention to become so fluent that when you're in Paris, Parisians mistake you as one of them and launch into long and complicated conversations with you in French? Make your French-learning promise specific.

Once you're specific about your promise to learn French, make a promise about specific steps you'll take to accomplish this. Promise, for example, to sign up at a local community college for the next available French class. Or promise to enroll in an online French course or buy a smartphone app to study on your own. And then promise to use those tools to study French language for, say, an hour a day, three days a week for the next three months.

Specificity also helps you be realistic about and comfortable with what you're promising. If there's a time dimension to it, for example, you'll need to be specific about the amount of time. Being realistic about time can be challenging in our hurry-up world where the assumption is made everything should be done in two seconds flat. We tend to underestimate just how much time something will take and fail to consider everything else we're already spending time on. Then, when we can't do everything we want to do in the amount of time we have, we feel frustrated and get upset with ourselves.

Bill Bartmann, in a "What's Your Promise?" interview for this book, shared the story of making a very specific promise that enabled him to triumph over what could have been a lifelong tragedy...

WHAT'S YOUR PROMISE?

Bill Bartmann's Promise to Walk Again

Bill Bartmann is the epitome of the self-made man. Born to a dirt-poor family, he would go on to become a millionaire and then a billionaire. But not before he hit rock-bottom, where he would discover the magic of making a promise.

Bill wrote about that amazing turning point in his life in his book, "Billionaire Secrets to Success." When he was 17 – a high school dropout and alcoholic – he fell down a staircase in a drunken stupor, crushing two vertebrae in his spinal cord and rupturing a disc. He was instantly paralyzed from the waist down. For the next six months, he was confined to a hospital bed, immobilized in traction.

"One day," he recalled, "my parents, our family doctor, Dr. Moberly, and our parish priest visited me in my hospital room. Dr. Moberly proceeded to tell a very frightened 17-year-old kid … that the paralysis was permanent and that I would never walk again." His parish priest told him that if this was God's will, he needed to accept it.

But Bill's reaction was anything but accepting. Instead, he violently rejected the idea that he would never walk again, yelling that he would not be a "cripple." But his doctor insisted, explaining that the spinal cord cannot heal itself after a significant trauma. That night, Bill cried himself to sleep.

Several hours later, he awoke alone in his dark room.

"It was in that dark hospital that I, for the first time in my life, made a promise to myself," he said. "In spite of everything Dr. Moberly had told me about my physical condition and the injury I had sustained, *I promised myself that I was going to walk out of that hospital under my own power.*"

With a newfound source of strength and resolve, he threw himself into physical therapy, expanding upon the minimal therapy the nurses offered. He determined to wiggle his toes by sheer willpower, practicing hour after hour, day after day until, incredibly, his toes moved. But when he told Dr. Moberly and even demonstrated it, the doctor's response was to inform him this was a medical impossibility and remind him that he would never, ever regain the ability to walk. And Bill began to doubt himself.

"That night, as I lay in bed feeling sorry for myself and verging on accepting life as a paraplegic, I remembered the promise I made to myself two weeks earlier," he recalled. "Every drop of medical science, every opinion of the medical staff, and every test were 100% consistent. The damage to my spinal cord was irreversible."

As he thought about the two conflicting propositions – that the medical science was clear, he would never walk again, versus his promise to himself that he would walk out of the hospital – he had a life-changing epiphany. "It was then and there that I realized my promise to myself was just as important as a mountain of medical evidence."

He secretly continued his toe-wiggling exercises and invented new ones that he practiced determinedly: Moving his body, inch by slow inch, down toward the foot of the bed. Bending and straightening his legs. Finally, he managed to sit up, push himself out of the bed, stand up and walk to the door of his room, leaving the nurses astounded.

"Two weeks later, I walked out of the hospital on my own power." He had fulfilled his promise!

Bill went on to finish high school, go to college and law school, and form a law practice specializing in consumer bankruptcy. Pursuing entrepreneurial interests, he built multi-million-dollar businesses in real estate and oil drilling. And then he took on a personal mission to reform the debt collection industry, playing a key role in new laws that require debt collectors to follow stringent practices to protect consumers, efforts that led to his nomination for the 2013 Nobel Peace Prize.

All rather unlikely accomplishments, some might say, for a former high school dropout who was supposed to be paralyzed for the rest of his life. But as he said of his epiphany in the hospital about the power of his promise, "I learned that outcomes are not always determined by knowledge or education or the capacity to perform logical analysis. Instead, sometimes outcomes are determined by the strength of a person's belief system."

Bill Bartmann's Nine Steps for Achieving Any Goal

Bartmann's personal experience with the power of turning a goal into a promise led him to develop a 9-step program for achieving any goal. I'll summarize these nine steps here. Notice the central role that making a promise plays in Bartmann's 9 Steps to Achieve Any Goal.

1. Make sure the goal you are setting for yourself is really your own goal.
2. Make It a ***Promise.***
3. Clearly Identify Your ***Promise.***
4. Identify Your Personal Motivator.
5. Create a ***Promise*** Plan.
6. Review Your Plan Regularly.
7. Tell Yourself You Will Achieve It.
8. Tell Others About Your ***Promise***.
9. Visualize the Final Result.

[My emphasis throughout.]

QUICK NOTE: MAKING A PROMISE SPECIFIC ALSO MEANS MAKING IT EXPLICIT

There is a vital difference between explicit and implicit promises. Bartmann's promise to himself was extremely explicit. You should always ask yourself: Are you making an explicit promise? Or is it implicit? Be careful! The most powerful promises can't be implicit. They must be made explicit. Why? Because with an explicit promise you're holding yourself accountable. Your integrity is on the line. Whereas an implicit promise is ambiguous and can lead to serious misunderstandings and disappointments.

As I mentioned in Chapter 2 (Ya Promise?), I think we would do well to reclaim the healthy tendency we had as kids to ask, "Ya promise?" when somebody told us they were going to do something. That question essentially asks for an explicit promise.

We all like to give ourselves a little ethical wiggle room. I get it. It's human nature. You might tell a co-worker, "Sure, I'll join you at the Monday meeting." Or you tell friends, "Let's play tennis this Saturday." But then, as the day approaches, or even at the last minute on that very day, you decide you'd rather not, and you pull a "no-show." You might even tell yourself it's okay because, after all, you never uttered the magic words, "I promise." Nonetheless, your words very well led others to expect that you were making a commitment, not just thinking about maybe going.

Powerful promises can't be implicit.
They must be made explicit.

I highly recommend that you challenge yourself by asking the sobering "Ya promise?" question before you make a commitment. This will help to clarify your level of commitment. And it's perfectly okay to be ambiguous if you're not 100% committed. It's better to say something like, "You know, I'd really like to be there but I'm not sure I can promise. Let me think about it and get back to you." This way, the other person doesn't walk away thinking you've made an explicit promise to meet at the meeting or play tennis. If, on the other hand, you're firmly committed and you feel comfortable saying "I promise," then do so.

If the commitment being made is taken to be a promise, this has enormous emotional importance. To avoid confusion and needless disappointment and even resentment in our personal and professional lives, it's always better to clarify whether you're making a promise. It's better to make your promises explicit and not leave room for ambiguity or misinterpretation by others. Get in the habit of saying "I Promise" when you mean it and be careful not to imply that you're making a promise when that's not your intention. If someone puts you on the spot and asks, "Ya promise?" (which I encourage you and others to do more often), be sure to respond honestly, with integrity, one way or the other.

[Author's Note: I plan to create some products related to this "Ya Promise?" idea. Perhaps some Ya Promise? tee-shirts. Ya Promise? wristbands. And Ya Promise? coffee mugs. Those kinds of things. I like the idea of popularizing the question – Ya Promise? – and putting people on the spot. Are you making an explicit promise or are you just implying that you're going to do something or go somewhere? Inquiring minds want to know.]

TIP 4: COMMIT EMOTIONALLY

"What comes from the heart goes to the heart," wrote the poet Samuel Coleridge. As mentioned numerous times already, I believe what differentiates a promise from a goal or an objective is the heart factor. Make sure you commit emotionally – that you put your heart into it – and you're virtually certain to keep your promise.

Making a promise engages your heart in the process. Making a promise to someone you care about makes you accountable to someone else in a special way. And your integrity is on the line with a promise. If you can, be sure to look that person in the eye and say the two magic words: "I promise."

If it's a promise to yourself, look at yourself in the mirror and say: "I promise." If your promise is to God (or some other deity or higher power) or to a loved one who is deceased, you should use your imagination. Imagine that you're looking this entity or person in the eye and say the two magic words: I Promise. The more detailed and clear you can make this image of looking somebody in the eye and making this promise, the more emotion you'll be able to attach to the promise. This could make all the difference in your determination to keep your word.

Former President Bill Clinton made a heartfelt promise to his daughter Chelsea before her 2010 wedding that he would take better care of himself by exercising more, watching his diet and losing weight. This promise didn't come out of the blue. It followed a major health scare when he underwent quadruple bypass surgery in 2004. Clinton made radical changes in his lifestyle, becoming a vegan, walking regularly and losing about 30 pounds.

It makes perfect sense to make a promise to someone we care about. That way we can enlist them in helping us keep our promise. It's like calling in reinforcements. A promise made to someone we care about makes us more accountable. I think Susan Boyle realized that she picked the one person in the world she cared most about – her beloved mother – knowing she could never allow herself to break a promise to her mother. Susan knew she had a gift. She knew she had a talent that could bring joy to others: her amazing singing voice. So, making the promise to her mother was, on some subconscious level, a way for Susan to commit emotionally to bringing out this talent into the world.

It's a smart strategy. I think I pursued a similar strategy on a subconscious level when I made the promise to my mother about writing HabitForce! – my first self-help book. It was a way to lock myself into doing something I may have sensed was a good idea, but I was not prepared to embrace the idea on a conscious level.

PROMISES ARE HEART CENTERED

It's worth restating here that a promise is much more powerful than antiseptic-sounding, cerebral words like "goal," "objective," "intention," "decision," "declaration," or "resolution." Making a promise engages your heart in the process. Making a promise to someone you care about makes you accountable to someone else in a special way. And your integrity is on the line with a promise

Even enhanced goal-setting techniques lack the essential ingredient that makes promise-making much more powerful. This ingredient, the heart factor, is discussed in detail later in this chapter. This is the notion that a promise comes from the heart and inherently involves a degree of emotional attachment to keeping the promise. Call it "heart-centered" goal setting.

Bill Bartmann's promise to walk again – and his system of turning goals into promises – is a terrific example of a heart-centered, emotion-filled promise. It also falls into a category of promises that I like to call "personal empowerment promises." These can truly be life changing.

Another example of a heart-centered, personal empowerment promise in action involves the young Theodore Roosevelt. At the age of twelve, Teddy made a heartfelt promise to his father that he would strengthen his body. He declared: "I will make my body," thereby expressing his determination to overcome his asthma and other frailties that plagued him during his childhood. This personal empowerment promise at an early age began a lifelong commitment to physical fitness and various forms of robust physical activity leading up to, during, and after his years serving as President of the United States.

TIP 5: WRITE IT

Writing down all your promises, even if you only make a few of them, will help you keep your word. The act of writing itself helps to clarify the promise. It helps to make it concrete and real. Particularly if you incorporate the two magic words – "I Promise" – at the beginning of each promise. It's essential that you do so. Always say and write those two magic words. This helps to make the promise explicit and avoids the confusion that can arise from an implicit or unclear promise.

Writing it down also helps you keep track of your promises. Don't rely on your memory when it comes to promises. They're too important, too precious to risk letting a promise slip your mind. All these tips taken together will help to make sure that doesn't happen. But writing down the promise, preferably in your Promise Journal so you will have easy and frequent access to it, will enhance the power of the promise. And writing the promise repeatedly will also help.

I created a special "I Promise" form that you can print. Please see the Resources section in the back of the book for more information about this form and other resources for making and keeping promises. I encourage you to use the "I Promise" form to write your promises and make them "official." You can also use mobile devices, electronic calendars and apps to write down and keep track of your promises. But be sure to keep a centralized record of all your promises. Ideally that would be your Promise Journal.

Martina Navratilova's Promise to Play Doubles with Pam Shriver

(https://www.martinanavratilova.com)
(https://www.pamelashriver.com)

As an avid tennis player and fan of the sport, I have always loved this story about the importance of writing down a promise: In 1985, tennis great Martina Navratilova made a promise – in writing – to continue playing doubles with Pam Shriver, a less-heralded but nonetheless very accomplished play, especially in doubles. The pair had just won their 100th straight match together and Navratilova told Shriver that she "was the only partner [she] ever wanted."

Shriver seemed to know instinctively that writing down a promise, and even signing your name to it, was a powerful way to codify Navratilova's commitment. So, Shriver wrote the following promise on a napkin and Navratilova promptly signed it. The note read: "I, Martina Navratilova, promise to always play doubles with Pam Shriver."

Navratilova kept the promise and together the team amassed a record-tying 20 Grand Slam titles over a 10-year period. At one stretch, they won 109 matches in a row, a record that is unlikely ever to be broken.

Writing a promise down and signing your name to it is a good way to strengthen the promise. This will help you to follow through and keep your word.

TIP 6: SHARE IT

If you really want to increase your chances of keeping your promise, share it with others. You can do that by making a promise to someone you care about (one of the "who-to's" described in Chapter 3) or you can make your promise public in some way. You could hold a promise-making ceremony to tell several friends and relatives about your promise at the same time.

I suggest in Chapter 7 that we try creating new promise-related traditions. For instance, you might want to consider making a promise on your birthday when you're celebrating with friends and relatives. In the United States we have a tradition of blowing out candles on a cake and making a wish on our birthdays. Why not make a public promise and then blow out the candles? Surely a promise is more powerful than a wish!

If you make a promise to someone you care about – as I did when I made the promise to my mother or when Teddy Roosevelt promised his father he would make his body stronger – you have shared the promise with at least another person. But it's a good idea to take this a step further. Bill Bartmann also recommends sharing your promise with others. Step 8 in his nine-step system for achieving any goal is to "Tell others about your promise."

In Chapter 7 I discuss in detail how I made a public promise – as a guest on several radio programs and in my public presentations – to share the power of promises with millions of people around the world. That public commitment has kept me motivated to finish writing this book and taking other steps to fulfill that public promise.

"Sometimes it takes a village to keep a promise."

Sharing your promise with one person or many is a way to call in reinforcements – witnesses and supporters – whose engagement with, and attachment to, your promise will help you persevere in keeping your word even when you might be tempted to give up and throw in the towel. Sharing elicits caring and support from those who know about your promise. Those to whom you made the promise – and those who are privileged to know about your promise – will feel like they have some skin in the game. So, they will do what they can to help you keep your promise. By sharing the promise with others, you make them part of your "Promise Community." Sometimes it takes a village to keep a promise.

In Chapter 7 you'll find more detail about creating a promise community – both in-person or online. You can also make use of social media like Facebook, X (formerly Twitter) or YouTube. Post your promise on your blog or website. The more people you tell about your promise, the more likely it is that you'll keep your word.

I mentioned this earlier, but I think this story bears repeating. An article about basketball legend LeBron published in the January 2025 issue of Cleveland Magazine, underscores the power of making your promise public. The article states: "LeBron James wears a rubber band on his wrist… the bracelet carries a bold statement: I Promise. The message reminds the superstar athlete of his mission — the one that's bigger than his goals on the court. His promise to uplift the community that made him."

So, LeBron James made a bold promise to himself, and he wears a rubber band on his wrist as a personal reminder and to proclaim his promise to the world.

Wearing one of my *PromisePower* Bands on your wrist is another way to make your promise public. When people ask about your *PromisePower* Band, you can explain why you're wearing it. It's a great conversation piece and an easy way to publicly reinforce your promise. To keep abreast of updates about these *PromisePower* wristbands by visiting the Resources page of this book.

The Promise That Launched Alcoholics Anonymous

Alcoholics Anonymous (AA), a self-help fellowship which has empowered millions of people all over the world to free themselves from the ravages of alcoholism, began with a shared promise.

In 1935, New York stockbroker Bill Wilson and Dr. Bob Smith, a surgeon from Akron, Ohio – both "hopeless alcoholics," as AA history puts it – promised each other that they would stop drinking would help each other remain abstinent from alcohol for the rest of their lives. What's more, they would invite other struggling alcoholics to join them in this journey by holding meetings on a regular basis to provide mutual support. This led to the establishment of AA meetings and the creation of the "12 Steps of Alcoholics Anonymous" and other guiding principles that provide ongoing comfort and inspiration.

That Bill Wilson and Dr. Bob's triumphed over their alcoholism, and the triumph repeated by millions who have followed in their footsteps, has everything to do with the shared promise at the center of AA. This fellowship makes clear that making a promise and keeping it is often a team effort, and there's no shame in that. The achievement of abstinence from alcohol is not diminished in the slightest when AA members share their promise with others and receive moral or emotional support in the process. In fact, Step 12 of AA's "12 Steps" contains a promise to "carry this message to alcoholics," in the knowledge that sharing one's success helps others succeed as well.

AA members also benefit from the kind of "start small" approach described in my Tip #1 for making and keeping promises. Approaching abstinence as a "One Day at a Time" effort transforms the goal of lifetime abstinence – a pretty darn daunting goal – into the smaller, more doable daily promise. A "clean and sober" friend of mine told me she probably couldn't have accomplished this if not for AA's "One Day at a Time" mantra.

"If I had told myself way back at my first AA meeting that I'd have to stop drinking for the rest of my life, I would have felt so overwhelmed that I probably would have headed straight to a bar after the meeting," she joked. "But not drinking one day at a time I could handle, and today I'm pleased to say it's been more than 30 years!"

TIP 7: FOLLOW THROUGH

Now we come to the single most important thing: You must follow through on the promises you make, whether they are large or small. You must "Keep Your Word," as I've titled

Chapter 5, which is entirely devoted to this subject. One hint: because the power of making a promise is ingrained in us from childhood, I strongly recommend that you make a promise to keep your promises. You should follow these tips for keeping the promise to keep promises, especially writing it down, sharing it, and committing emotionally.

You'll see that this promise to keep your promises is the final promise in the "Promise a Day" program included at the end of Chapter 6.

Please take another look at these seven tips. Write these down in your Promise Journal. If possible, you should commit these tips to memory. They are specifically designed for easy recall.

7 TIPS FOR MAKING AND KEEPING PROMISES

1. Start Small
2. Be Selective
3. Be Specific
4. Commit Emotionally
5. Write It
6. Share It
7. Follow Through

To learn more about the importance of following through on your promises, and to learn about specific tips to help you keep your promises, let's move onto Chapter 5. I promise this chapter will provide you with useful insights that will boost your integrity and help you keep your word.

"I made a promise to Madiba, and I intend to keep it."
- Oprah Winfrey on her promise to Nelson Mandela

CHAPTER 5

Keep Your Word: Tips for Making and Keeping Promises

Following through on your promises
Insights and tips for boosting your *PromisePower*

THE POWER OF A HUMBLE RUBBER BAND

Now to the single most important tenet of promises: You must keep them. The rich rewards of your promises are yours when you keep your word, follow through, do what you say you will do.

"This is where the rubber meets the road" began the previous chapter, "Make a Promise."

Well, *this* chapter is where you shift into gear and get moving in the direction of your promise and keep moving. No matter what roadblocks or detours you might encounter along the way, you maneuver around them or through them and you keep on moving, *because you promised.*

Let's take a moment to remember where we are in the four-stage booster rockets we've covered already. We have reached the second element in the four part mantra:

Make a Promise.
KEEP YOUR WORD.
Change Your Life.
Transform the World.

In this chapter we will consider several ideas and strategies designed to help you keep your word. We can take heart from Jack Canfield's assertion in his foreword that "A promise is a promise!" This is a very good place to start as you consider ways to fortify yourself against any temptation to backslide on your promises.

Once, when I was being interviewed on a radio program about the power of promises, an elementary school teacher called in to the show. She described an encounter she had with one of her students. The teacher had promised the class that they would take a field trip on a specific day. The teacher's schedule later became crowded, and she told the class they would have to skip the field trip. Then one of her students said: "But you promised!" The teacher was taken aback. The little girl was right. The teacher *had* promised. Recognizing that a promise is a promise, the teacher relented, and the class went on the field trip after all. And the teacher felt much better because she kept her promise.

A promise is a promise. That's the message of Oprah Winfrey's promise to Nelson Mandela. I referred to Oprah's promise in Chapter 1, but I want to share it with you again because it relates directly to keeping your word.

WHAT'S YOUR PROMISE?

Oprah Winfrey's Promise to Build a School for Girls in South Africa

On a visit to South Africa in 2000, Oprah Winfrey made a promise to Nelson Mandela that she would build an academy for underprivileged girls in South Africa. She pledged to donate $10 million for the project. When it was finally completed in 2007, the Oprah Winfrey Leadership Academy for Girls had cost Oprah $40 million. The campus consists of 28 buildings including computer and science laboratories, a wellness center, a library and a theater.

Despite cost overruns and other complications, Oprah was determined to keep her promise. In the middle of the project she explained to CNN why she didn't abandon the costly project: "I made a promise to Madiba (Mandela's nickname), and I intend to keep it."

That, in a nutshell, is the power of making a promise. In just a few short words, Oprah crystallizes the unique power of a promise. There is an emotional charge, a level of commitment and a burning determination that simply doesn't exist with traditional methods of setting goals or stating intentions. Notice that Oprah did not say: "I set a goal, and I intend to achieve it." Or "I made a resolution, and I intend to do it." There is a powerful, gut-level connection between the words "promise" and "keep" – as is elaborated on in this chapter.

In Chapter 1, I quoted Brian Tracy, a leading sales training authority and bestselling author who wrote: "Leaders know that honesty and integrity are the foundations of leadership. Leaders keep their promises."

To quote his elaboration of that thought: *"Always keep your word. Be a person of honor.* **If you say that** *you will do something, do it. If you make a promise, keep it.* **If you** *make a commitment, fulfill it. Be known as the kind of person that can be trusted absolutely, no matter what the circumstances."*

The point here is that all successful people, not just businesspeople, can be counted on to keep their promises. I use "successful" here not in the narrow sense related to money or external power. I mean successful in the broadest possible sense. Successful as a human being, as someone who has deep personal power, absolute integrity and a strong character.

Think about the last promise you made to someone. Maybe you said: "Yes, honey, I'll take out the trash after dinner." But did you deliver? Or did you renege?

Or maybe you said (or received) a promise like this: "I promise we'll give you a promotion in six months."

Perhaps you made this common promise: "I'll be there. I promise."

If you are like most people, you make commitments to others all the time. Question is, how often do you keep them? It's a good idea to take stock of how often you fail to keep your word, and how you handle it when you do. This is key to understanding yourself. And self-awareness is key to personal change.

When we don't keep a promise to someone, it communicates to that person that we don't value him or her. We have chosen to put something else ahead of our commitment. Even when we break small promises, others learn that they cannot count on us. Tiny fissures develop in our relationships when we don't keep our word, and those fissures can turn into big cracks and even complete breaks over time.

We are not only communicating to other people that our word can't be trusted. We are also telling *ourselves* that we don't value our own word. We think it is okay to let someone down, to say something we don't mean, or to fail to follow through on something we said we would do. Not keeping a promise is the same as disrespecting yourself. Ultimately, it can harm our self-image, our self-esteem, our relationships, and our life.

Let's face it. Keeping promises isn't always easy. Hence the need for this chapter devoted to keeping your word after making a promise. We are all blessed with incredible powers of body, mind and spirit. But things get complicated because our body, mind and spirit aren't always synced up. Result? We sometimes think one thing and do another, despite the best of intentions. We have conflicting feelings. We see the path we want to take but head in the opposite direction – often driven by habits that we're comfortable with but also habits that may not serve us.

Things aren't always as clear as we'd like them to be, and we're not always as in charge of ourselves as we imagine ourselves to be. There is also a tendency to seek refuge in excuses, to point fingers at circumstances or other people to explain why we had to abandon the best-laid plans and goals and, on occasion, even some promises.

This chapter is all about steeling yourself against backsliding and reneging on your make-or-break promises.

Political theorist and historian, Hannah Arendt, said: "The remedy for unpredictability, for the chaotic uncertainty of the future, is contained in the faculty to make and keep promises."

Oprah's story illustrates this point. She was determined to complete the school project because she made a promise. That promise made the future more predictable and less chaotic. Others could rely on what Oprah promised. They weren't left to wonder whether she would follow through.

Oprah herself recognized that her integrity was on the line. She was also bolstered in keeping her word because of the recipient of the promise – Nelson Mandela – someone she and hundreds of millions of people around the world respected, even revered. So, in this case, Oprah's promise was made to someone she cared deeply about. And that helped to keep her committed to following through and keeping her word.

MAKE A PROMISE TO KEEP YOUR PROMISES

This may sound corny, but I want to suggest a simple, proactive, personal empowerment strategy that will bolster your commitment from the very start: I urge you to make a heartfelt promise – right now – to keep your promises. In addition, you should become an advocate for others – friends, loved ones and colleagues – to keep their promises, too. This creates something of a mutual support group. So, here's a proposed promise that could help you keep your word:

I promise to keep my promises, and
I encourage others to keep their promises, too.

You will find this promise at the very end of Chapter 6. This promise to keep promises is the culminating promise of a program I created called "30 Days to a Promising Future." I developed that program to help you build a promise-a-day habit into your schedule for 30 days straight.

VISUALIZE YOURSELF KEEPING YOUR PROMISES

You will also give your commitment a boost by visualizing promise-keeping. Numerous studies have shown that visualization – a kind of mental rehearsal of actions and their desired results – is quite powerful in helping everyone – from athletes to actors and businesspeople – succeed.

A form of visualization is built into the Alcoholics Anonymous program in a series of statements known as "The 12 Promises" and read aloud at meetings. An AA member friend of mine told me that repeatedly hearing these promises and their vivid descriptions of the rewards to be had in stopping drinking has played a big part in her 30-plus years of sobriety:

"If we are painstaking about this phase of our development, we will be amazed before we are halfway through. We are going to know a new freedom and a new happiness. We will not regret the past nor wish to shut the door on it. We will comprehend the word serenity, and we will know peace. No matter how far down the scale we have gone, we will see how our experience can benefit others. That feeling of uselessness and self-pity will disappear. We will lose interest in selfish things and gain interest in our fellows. Self-seeking will slip away. Our whole attitude and outlook upon life will change. Fear of people and of economic insecurity will leave us. We will intuitively know how to handle situations which used to baffle us. We will suddenly realize that God is doing for us what we could not do for ourselves. Are these extravagant promises? We think not. They are being fulfilled among us – sometimes quickly, sometimes slowly. They will always materialize if we work for them."

The following Inward Bound self-awareness exercise, which makes use of visualization, is invaluable. Greater clarity, unearthing new levels of self-awareness through introspection, will help in your promise-keeping journey. So, I invite you to spend a few minutes on this powerful visualization exercise. First, read through the exercise below and then think about some of the questions and issues raised during your meditation.

INWARD BOUND

Explore Keeping a Promise

Sit or lie down in a comfortable, quiet place where you won't be disturbed for about 30 minutes. Close your eyes. Take three to five deep, relaxing breaths, in and out slowly.

Think about a promise you'd like to make. It could be a promise to yourself, to someone you care about or to a higher power. It could be something small that pops into your mind as you do this exercise, or it could be an important goal you've had for quite some time but haven't steadfastly pursued.

Now imagine yourself making your promise. Notice: Who are you making this promise to? Yourself? Someone else? God or a higher power? And what words do you use in making your promise?

Notice how you feel when you make your promise. Maybe you're happy or excited. But maybe what you're feeling is something else – not feeling very confident, perhaps, maybe even feeling some fear or anxiety. If negative feelings like these come up, try redirecting the promise to yourself or someone else and see how that feels.

Visualize yourself following through on your promise:

- What are some of the first steps you take to follow through? What changes in your life do you make?
- How are your life and the lives of others changed by keeping this promise?
- How does it feel to keep your promise?

As you conclude this exercise, slowly return your awareness to the room you're in and open your eyes. Chances are good that you had some fresh and perhaps even surprising insights. Make notes about your feelings and insights in your Promise Journal to "lock in" their lessons and have them available for future reference.

MAKE PROMISE-KEEPING A HABIT

How easy we find it to keep our promises – or how difficult – comes down to one thing: Our promise-keeping habits, from habits of thought to behavioral habits. In this chapter and the next, you'll learn to take charge and build habits of thought and action that will empower you to keep the promises you make and, ultimately, reap the rich rewards of doing so.

Life is complicated. And we're all complicated beings with different motivations, values and habits. As I discuss in more detail in Chapter 6, habits are key to keeping – or breaking – promises. Some of the ideas below will help you break through the complications. In fact, I think making and keeping promises is one way to simplify things. There's nothing simpler or more powerful than this: A promise is a promise. It's make-or-break.

When it comes to promises, it's a good idea to follow the K.I.S.S. formula: "Keep It Simple, Stupid." Or, to reword the old saying: "Keep It Simple, Silly."

Remember, whenever you make a promise your integrity is on the line. You must follow through. Make a solemn promise to yourself, to a higher power, or to someone you care about – or all three at once! – to keep your word!

REVIEW THE 7 TIPS FROM CHAPTER 4

Several of the tips from the previous chapter have a direct bearing on your ability to follow through and keep your word. I encourage you to review those tips and any insights you gleaned from them that could help in keeping your word. Starting small, being selective, being specific, committing emotionally, writing down your promise and sharing it – all these tips can be harnessed to help you follow through. You should be sure to read anything you wrote in your Promise Journal about these 7 tips.

READ THE PROMISES YOU WROTE DOWN

This is the natural follow-up step after the "Write It" tip for making a promise. Putting a verbal promise in writing notches up your level of commitment. To take things up yet another notch, *read* your written-down promises. Don't just write them down and file them away where you'll never see them again. Be sure to keep your promises front-and-center.

For example, use your Promise Journal to write down all your promises and keep them together in one place. Then, on a daily basis, pull out your Promise Journal and read your promises. Better yet, read each promise aloud. This helps you form a deeper bond with your promises by stimulating the speech-processing parts of your brain, integrating your promise right into your brain's neuronal pathways.

Read your promises slowly, savoring each word, and with feeling. If your promise is one you've made to someone you love (this could be yourself, another person or even a higher power), close your eyes and feel your love swelling and warming your heart. Remember, promises are heart-centered so put your heart into it at every opportunity.

Here are more ways to read and otherwise see your promises in writing:

- Write each of your promises on a small index card, keep the cards together with a rubber band or in an envelope, and keep this on your bedside table, in your wallet or purse or some other place where seeing it automatically reminds you of your promises.
- Write your promises on colorful sticky-notes and affix these to your refrigerator door, bathroom mirror and any other place where you'll see them over the course of your day.
- Create a screensaver of your promises – just one promise or several – that you can display on your computer, phone and other digital device where screensavers or other background images pop up automatically many times a day. You probably already use a custom screensaver (and I wager that you or someone you know has a screensaver image of a beautiful scene from nature or cute kittens), so why not use a screensaver that inspires you by reminding you of your heartfelt promises?

MAKE A PLAN FOR KEEPING YOUR PROMISES

It will help if you create a concrete plan to fulfill the promise. Be careful not to neglect smaller promises. All promises should be fulfilled. You don't need to make this complicated. Just think about and develop a step-by-step plan for keeping your word. How do you plan to make this happen?

It's possible your promise will require some effort or attention every day. Let's say your promise is about getting exercise or losing weight, for instance. You'll need to schedule time to keep that promise, either every day or certainly a few times a week. Otherwise, the promise will be neglected, and you'll be playing catch up or you'll just give up. Don't let that happen. Remember, the first tip from the previous chapter. It's perfectly okay to Start Small. Make a promise or two that you can comfortably fulfill and create a simple plan of action to do so.

WEAR IT (AND SHARE IT)

Carry your promises with you wherever you go by wearing a reminder. While this could mean something dramatic such as a T-shirt emblazoned with your promise word-for-word, I suggest something more subtle: a promise-reminder on your wrist. A lightweight, inexpensive wristband will do. You can order and wear a *PromisePower* wristband (details to be announced later). Even if all you do is occasionally spot your wristband out of the corner of your eye or feel it ever-so-slightly pressing against your skin, every one of these tiny moments of contact will be sending a message to your brain about how important your promises are to you.

This is also a good way to enlist the power boost of sharing your promise – one of the 7 tips for making a promise in Chapter 4. When other people happen to spot your wristband, they might ask you about it, giving you an opportunity to share as much (or as little) about your promise as you'd like. This reinforces your commitment because now someone else is in on your promise with you. Not that you're looking for "enforcers," but people with whom you've shared your promise will often start caring about your promise right along with you. And don't be surprised if sharing your promise with someone prompts them to tell you about *their* promises, and before you know it you've got a promise-keeping, two-person "support group" going.

Share your promises with a friend. Research recently conducted about reaching goals by Psychology Professor Gail Matthews showed that people who wrote down their goals, shared this information with a friend, and sent weekly updates to that friend were on average 33% more successful in accomplishing their stated goals than those who merely formulated goals. I believe the same principles apply to keeping promises. Write them down. Share them. And keep your friends and loved ones updated about your progress.

THE POWER OF A HUMBLE RUBBER BAND

A simple variation on the *PromisePower* wristband is a common, everyday rubber band you can wear on your wrist. This is a remarkably effective tool for reminding yourself of your promises – and a whole lot more.

In fact, I happen to think a humble rubber band is perhaps the most powerful personal empowerment device ever invented in human history. That might sound like hyperbole, but I firmly believe it. In my Personal Empowerment Programs (PEPTalks), I often pass out a rubber band for participants to wear on their wrists. This serves three purposes.

First, as mentioned, the band serves as a constant reminder of a promise that you've made. Having this reminder constantly on your wrist is invaluable.

Second, a rubber band also serves a helpful metaphor for what I call HabitForce, the power of habits to determine what we accomplish or fail to accomplish in our lives. The limp rubber band represents how we feel with our existing collection of habits. We are at ease with our habits. This is our comfort zone. When you make a promise, set a goal or try to make any changes in your life, your HabitForce stretches like a rubber band. Far too often it *snaps back* to its previous, stress-free state. The limp band on your wrist reminds you of the dangers of snapping back to your existing habits and breaking your promise.

Third, the rubber band can be used to help you "snap out of it." What do I mean by that? Simple. HabitForce is such a powerful influence on our lives because it operates largely below the level of conscious awareness. We're comfortable with habits that have been programmed over a lifetime. That's why change and keeping promises can be difficult.

The change process is often sabotaged by our internal dialog, that nagging self-talk often dissuades us from making desired changes. I encourage you to use the rubber band to snap out of it – by giving yourself a SNAP of the rubber band when you become aware of a negative, disempowering, or undermining thought. You might even say to yourself: Why did I make that stupid promise anyway? I don't have to keep my promise. Who's going to care? Any negative thought along those lines that could lead you to break your promise deserve a hearty SNAP of the rubber band. Anytime you find yourself rationalizing how you could break your promise, give yourself a big SNAP with the rubber band.

This simple exercise will help you become aware of what that negative little voice is saying to you. Self-talk can serve you or unnerve you! It's your choice. Self-awareness is key to change. Over time, the mere act of becoming aware of negative thoughts, and giving yourself a *SNAP* every time—will condition your subconscious mind to avoid those disempowering thoughts and to replace them with positive, empowering thoughts. Thoughts are powerful things, and the rubber band technique is a simple but effective way to train your mind to think more positively and stay the course.

Look. Nobody's perfect. We must expect a few negative thoughts to pop into our heads now and then. People who succeed in life … people who keep their promises … find a way to recognize these negative thoughts, reject them consciously … and replace them with positive thoughts that help them reach their goals and keep their promises. It's simple, but that doesn't mean it's always easy. The rubber band technique can be a big help.

"Self-talk can serve you or unnerve you!"

TRACK YOUR PROGRESS AND CELEBRATE!

This is a close relative of the plan mentioned above. You want to keep track of the progress you're making toward fulfilling your promise. So, keep a written log in your Promise Journal. You can also track your progress on your online calendar if that's more convenient.

Be sure to reward yourself for keeping a promise. Celebrate. This doesn't have to be something big, expensive or even material. Sure, you could treat yourself to something special – a nice dinner or a movie. A day at the spa. Take a drive in the country. Or just take some time off to recharge your batteries. You could simply write "I did it!" on a piece of paper and tape it to your bathroom mirror. Make note of your success in your Promise Journal or calendar. Write in big, bold colors: "Promise kept!"

The important thing is to establish the habit of celebrating and valuing when you keep your promises. Every time. Make sure you reward yourself in some special way that tells you that you're proud of yourself. That you recognize that keeping that promise was an achievement worthy of celebration. And be sure to tell others that you kept your word. They will want to know about the fact that you honored your commitment. Those who care about you will want to share in your celebration.

Keeping your word, fulfilling your promises is the right thing to do. It doesn't have to be more complicated than that. It makes you feel good about yourself. It strengthens your self-esteem and your sense of self-worth. It fortifies your promise-making muscles, so you'll be better equipped to take on more goals and make more promises. Keeping your word is key to your ability to Believe More in yourself, Achieve More in your life, and Receive More of the good things that you want and deserve, not just in a selfish way but because you'll be able to Contribute More to your family, your community and the world at large.

Now turn to Chapter 6 for exciting personal empowerment insights and tools you can use to harness the power of promises to change your life.

"The most powerful motivational speech in the world is what you say to yourself."

CHAPTER 6

Change Your Life: Make Promise-Keeping a Habit

Positive Self-Talk
Two Key Success Habits
The Six Axioms of Personal Empowerment
A Pep Talk in Every Promise: A Promise a Day – 30 Days to a Promising Future

TOP TEN PROMISES FOR A SUCCESSFUL LIFE

Now we come to the third element of the four-part mantra. Here's a reminder of the structure:

Make a Promise.
Keep Your Word.
CHANGE YOUR LIFE.
Transform the World.

In Chapters 4 and 5, you learned tips for making promises and keeping your word. In this chapter, you'll learn about several personal empowerment tools that will help you change your life.

Doing so requires, first and foremost, that you make a habit of keeping your promises. And for that to happen, you need to leverage time-tested methods for psyching yourself up and staying on track over time.

POSITIVE SELF-TALK

Let's be clear. When it comes to making it a practice to consistently keep your promises and using that practice to change your life for the better, there's no substitute for positive self-talk. A negative mindset, practiced habitually, will sabotage your life-changing and promise-keeping efforts. What goes on between your ears determines what your life looks like and will either undermine or accelerate the positive changes you'd like to manifest in the world.

Here's the bottom line: The most powerful motivational speech in the world is what you say to yourself. This is the main reason I don't put much stock in the ability of so-called motivational speakers to provide the impetus for lasting change in our lives. Indeed, this truism echoes the Six Axioms of Personal Empowerment presented later in this chapter.

Great teachers throughout history have always appreciated the incredible power of our own thoughts to shape our destiny. We all have the power to become aware of, and to change, our thoughts. By doing so, we have the power to change our future. And the first step in the change process is to keep our promises.

The process of personal change begins with self-awareness. I encourage you to write down your positive and negative thoughts in a journal so you can detect the subtle messages you send to yourself. Are you sending positive, empowering messages, or negative, disempowering signals?

We should all spend a few minutes daily working on the inside. With personal growth and change, the onus is on you. You determine your destiny because you alone can control your thoughts and the actions that spring from your thoughts. Put simply: What we think is what we get!

SUCCESS IS AN INSIDE JOB

If you want to sum up my message in just a few words, they would be Success is an inside job. The late Lou Tice, founder of the Pacific Institute, makes this critical point in his personal excellence programs. He says that he spends a great deal of his time "working on the inside." What he means is that he visualizes his goals. He constructs and repeats positive statements or affirmations. He sees vividly the reality he wants to create in his mind's eye before he makes it happen. He paints a clear mental picture – a blueprint of the future – and then he proceeds to "grow into it."

The journey toward changing your life and keeping your promises is, first and foremost, an inward journey. A popular program called Outward Bound takes people on adventures of personal discovery out in nature. Think of changing your life as a kind of Inward Bound program in which the challenges you confront and overcome will largely be inside – your mindsets, attitudes, beliefs, internal dialogue, and habits of thought. Your promise-keeping mission is the ultimate inside job.

Joan's Promise to Learn to Play the Bassoon

This promise story underscores the importance of positive thinking and the unexpected positive consequences of making a promise. A friend of mine (I'll call her "Joan") told me about a life-changing promise she made. Joan's son had been playing the cello in a community orchestra for several years. And Joan, who attended all her son's performances and quite a few rehearsals, got to know his fellow musicians quite well.

When her son was about to leave their town for college, Joan told the other orchestra members that she would miss spending time with them. Well, they responded, Joan might be able join the orchestra herself if she played a musical instrument. Alas, she didn't. She'd learned a little piano as a child and could read music, and that was about it. But out of curiosity, she asked her musicians friends what instrument the orchestra needed. The bassoon, they said. While the orchestra had one bassoonist, it could use another.

And while she had never played anything close to a bassoon, Joan soon found herself promising the orchestra that she would learn to play the instrument and would join them. The fact that there was one other bassoon player, Joan told me, gave her confidence in knowing she would not be completely on her own.

Over the next four months, Joan dedicated hours and hours to learning the bassoon. At times, she confessed, she doubted whether it was worth the effort. But she reminded herself that she'd promised, so she persevered and made progress.

On the day of her first performance with the orchestra, Joan arrived with butterflies fluttering around in her stomach. On top of that, she learned that the other bassoonist was ill and wouldn't be able to perform. Joan said she was a "nervous wreck" because she was now the only bassoonist, and she had to perform a bassoon solo. She had to give herself a serious pep talk to go out there on stage. Her husband was in the audience, marveling at Joan's ability to perform very competently in front of an audience a mere four months after picking up the bassoon for the first time.

Afterwards, Joan said the experience was exhilarating for her. She said performing the solo successfully made her feel "like a schoolgirl who just turned her first cartwheel!" At age 59, Joan said she felt like a teenager again.

For Joan, her success at mastering the bassoon in short order truly was an inside job. She kept a positive mental attitude and expected only the best from herself. When doubts crept into her mind, she reminded herself of the promise she made. Joan also noticed that several additional benefits accompanied her making and fulfilling this promise. These unexpected benefits are the result of what I call the "karmic halo effect" of making and keeping your promises. Joan's promise to learn to play the bassoon brought her closer to her older brother, who is a percussionist for several orchestras. It is also bringing her closer to her cello-playing, 19-year-old son, who had to leave the orchestra for college. And Joan has begun to scout around for suitable community orchestras that might need a bassoonist when she decides to retire in the next few years.

So, this rather rash promise has changed Joan's life in many ways, large and small. It allowed her to feel a priceless sense of accomplishment and the exhilaration of performing solo in front of an audience. She felt like a teenager again. And she has made a positive contribution to the lives of people around her, including other members of the orchestra and the community at large. The positive benefits of making and keeping this promise are virtually impossible to measure.

THE SIX AXIOMS OF PERSONAL EMPOWERMENT

There is great wisdom in this Chinese proverb:
Sow a thought, reap an action.

Sow an action, reap a habit.
Sow a habit, reap a character.
Sow a character, reap a destiny.

Thoughts are powerful things that determine your destiny. The good news is that you can control your thoughts. You can train your mind to think more positively.

I developed the following Six Axioms of Personal Empowerment to underscore both the importance of habits in our lives and the critical role that thoughts play in shaping our habits. These axioms are a key personal empowerment tool. They are indispensable for anyone who wants to turn their lives around, achieve their goals and keep their promises.

You can read more about these Six Axioms and how they relate to harnessing your HabitForce and making the shift from what I call FAILURE habits to SUCCESS habits in my book titled, *Harness Your HabitForce.*

This kind of personal empowerment is also about personal fulfillment, even happiness. As mentioned earlier, the late President John F. Kennedy was fond of quoting what he called the ancient Greek definition of happiness: "The full use of your powers along lines of excellence." The Six Axioms can help you find that very happiness for yourself. Making the full use of your powers – through Habits, Promises, and Speaking – opens a brave new world of accomplishment, fulfillment, and happiness.

Put another way, when you go through life holding back, falling short of your potential, feeling frustrated and trapped, you're not making the full use of your powers along lines of excellence. As a result, I believe your personal power and your happiness are diminished.

These Six Axioms of Personal Empowerment can boost your ability to make promises and keep them. An axiom is a truism, something accepted without question as true. A self-evident or universally recognized truth, a statement (in mathematics often shown in symbolic form) so evident or well-established that it is accepted without controversy or question. I want you to accept these Six Axioms as truisms. If you do, you can use them – coupled with the power of making a promise – to change your life.

Most successful people seem to have been lucky enough to develop success-oriented HabitForce programming. Sadly, those who feel disempowered and fall short of their potential seem to have been programmed for failure, not success. Disempowered people have been saddled with self-defeating mental habits and counterproductive mindsets. If you sense that you might be one of those people – and we all are to some degree – understanding the following Six Axioms will go a long way toward helping you take charge of your HabitForce and reprogram your personal operating system for positive results.

AXIOM #1: *"WE ARE WHAT WE REPEATEDLY DO."*

This first axiom comes from Aristotle. The ancient Greek philosopher recognized the power of habits in shaping our lives. It's a powerful lesson for all of us. We often talk about the force of habit. I call this HabitForce. The poet Ovid also recognized the power of habits: "Nothing is more powerful than custom or habit." The poet John Dryden wrote: "Habits gather by unseen degrees, As brooks make rivers and rivers run to seas." The ability to change begins when we recognize the power of repeated patterns of thought and behavior. Aristotle went on to say that "excellence is not an act, but a habit."

The same can be said for failure. Football coach Vince Lombardi adds: "*Winning is a habit. Unfortunately, so is losing." Jim Ryun, the Olympic Silver Medalist and former member of Congress who broke the four-minute mile as a high school student, also believed in the power of habit. He said:* "Motivation is what gets you started. Habit is what keeps you going." And William James wrote, "All our life, as far as it has definite form, is but a mass of habits."

AXIOM #2: *HABITFORCE CAN EITHER WORK FOR YOU OR AGAINST YOU.*

Force of habit – what I call HabitForce – is neutral. It's a bit like gravity or any other law of physics. It just is. HabitForce can be positive or negative. It can either serve your purposes or it can work against you. HabitForce can be either insidious or empowering because it's so familiar and comfortable. This quote – attributed to theologian Nathanael Emmons – sums up the situation nicely: "Habit is either the best of servants, or the worst of masters."

Basically, HabitForce defines the boundaries of your comfort zones. You can either make a habit of success, or you can make a habit of failure. Either way, it takes the same amount of effort and energy. Our HabitForce gets programmed in our earliest years and simply runs, like a software program, on autopilot. HabitForce is your Personal Operating System. It operates on the subconscious level, which means we don't always know why we do what we do or why we can't easily change our existing patterns. Once you master how HabitForce works, you can use it to help you keep your promises.

AXIOM #3: *YOU HAVE A CHOICE. YOU CAN REPROGRAM YOUR HABITFORCE.*

The good news is your HabitForce software program isn't etched in stone. It may be your default programming, but it can be reprogrammed. That's the entire premise of this book. Unfortunately, we weren't issued a *User's Guide* for operating our HabitForce program when we were born. This book aims to change that. This is, in fact, the *User's Guide* for doing exactly that. There is a simple, three-step process for reprogramming your HabitForce, so it works for you, not against you.

I cover this process in greater detail in *Harness Your HabitForce*. I call it the Three Rs: *Recognize, Reject, and Replace*. This is what I refer to as the technology of personal change. You first need to *Recognize* the habits you'd like to change. You then must consciously *Reject* these habits – with strong emotion and commitment. Now you're able to *Replace* them with the corresponding positive habits that will help you achieve your goals and keep your promises.

AXIOM #4: *YOU CAN'T CHANGE WHAT YOU DON'T REALIZE.*

Self-awareness is key to the change process. More specifically, awareness of the power of HabitForce is critical in the change process. You can't implement the *Three Rs* unless you spend time in personal reflection and meditation. You must get very clear about the specific patterns that are holding you back and undermining your success. As mentioned already, the habits that hold people back take place "between the ears." These are patterns of thought that manifest in negative self-talk. Change begins when we manage to bring our negative internal dialogue – that nagging little voice in the back of your head – up to conscious awareness. Once we become aware of the negative messages we're sending ourselves, we're in a much better position to change those messages from self-defeating to empowering.

The great philosopher, Yoda from "Star Wars," said in his convoluted syntax: "Named must your fear be before banish it you can." Axiom 4 is essentially the same idea. You must name your negative habit before you can banish or change it. You simply can't change what you're unaware of. Awareness is empowering.

AXIOM #5: *"IT TAKES A HABIT TO REPLACE A HABIT."*

This insight comes from Napoleon Hill, author of the self-help classic *Think and Grow Rich.* Like Aristotle and many others, Hill recognized the power of habits. Hill wrote about something he called *Cosmic Habitforce.* He realized that you can't simply change a habit. You need to replace one habit with another habit. I believe this is where the change process usually breaks down. Lots of people want to make changes or establish a new habit in their lives, but they don't take the time to inventory their supply of existing negative habits.

Essentially, we have all the habits we need and can manage. We're full of habits. They help us get through our days by following established routines and even ruts. Think of it this way. It's as if you're packing for a trip and your suitcase is completely full. You simply can't cram one more item into the suitcase, but you really want to take your favorite sweater. It simply won't fit. What do you do? You must remove something from the suitcase to make room for that sweater. It's the same with habits. You must replace a habit with another habit. You can't simply add a new habit. That's why this book introduces those two seven-letter acronyms: FAILURE and SUCCESS. You can use the Three Rs to *Recognize* and *Reject* FAILURE habits and *Replace* them with their SUCCESS counterparts. Take it from Hill, it takes a habit to replace a habit.

AXIOM #6: *"WE BECOME WHAT WE THINK ABOUT."*

This quote comes from Earl Nightingale, the great personal development author, radio personality and speaker. He created a recording of what he called "The Strangest Secret in the World" in 1956. The recording sold more than a million copies almost immediately with virtually no publicity or advertising. In this recording, Nightingale reveals that the strangest secret is: "We become what we think about." He stated quite clearly that this single sentence, this secret, was the key to success, and the key to failure.

This profound truth – closely related to the Law of Attraction that was popularized in the hit movie and book "The Secret" – this profound truth has been recognized through the ages. Buddha said: "All that we are is the result of what we have thought. The mind is everything. What we think we become."

The same idea can be found in the Bible. "As a man thinketh in his heart, so is he." – Proverbs 23:7

James Allen, author of *As a Man Thinketh*, believed: "All that a man achieves and all that he fails to achieve is the direct result of his own thoughts."

As Roman Emperor and philosopher Marcus Aurelius wrote: "Our life is what our thoughts make it."

Psychologist and writer William James once observed that the greatest discovery of his generation was that "Human beings can alter their lives by altering their attitudes of mind."

Great teachers through the ages understood the incredible power of our own thoughts to shape our destiny. We all have the power to become aware of – and to change – our thoughts. By changing our thoughts, we have the power to change our future.

Henry David Thoreau wrote: "Thought is the sculptor who can create the person you want to be."

Napoleon Hill observed: "You become what you think about" and "Life reflects your own thoughts back to you." He also wrote this memorable line: "Whatever the mind can conceive and believe, it can achieve."

So, always remember: the most powerful motivational (or demotivational) speech in the world is what you say to yourself. Neville Goddard observed: "You create your future by your inner conversation."

So, monitor your thoughts. Keep track of what you say to yourself. Be careful what you spend your time thinking about. Your dominant, habitual thoughts will determine what you achieve – or fail to achieve. Sow a thought, reap a destiny.

A good exercise is to write down your positive and negative thoughts in a journal so you can get a better handle on the subtle messages you send to yourself. Are you sending positive, empowering messages or are you sending negative, disempowering signals?

Your thoughts become self-fulfilling prophecies, so you must choose them wisely. You will reap in the world what you first sow in your mind. In other words, what you think is what you get. If you program your HabitForce correctly, you'll find it much easier to make and keep important promises.

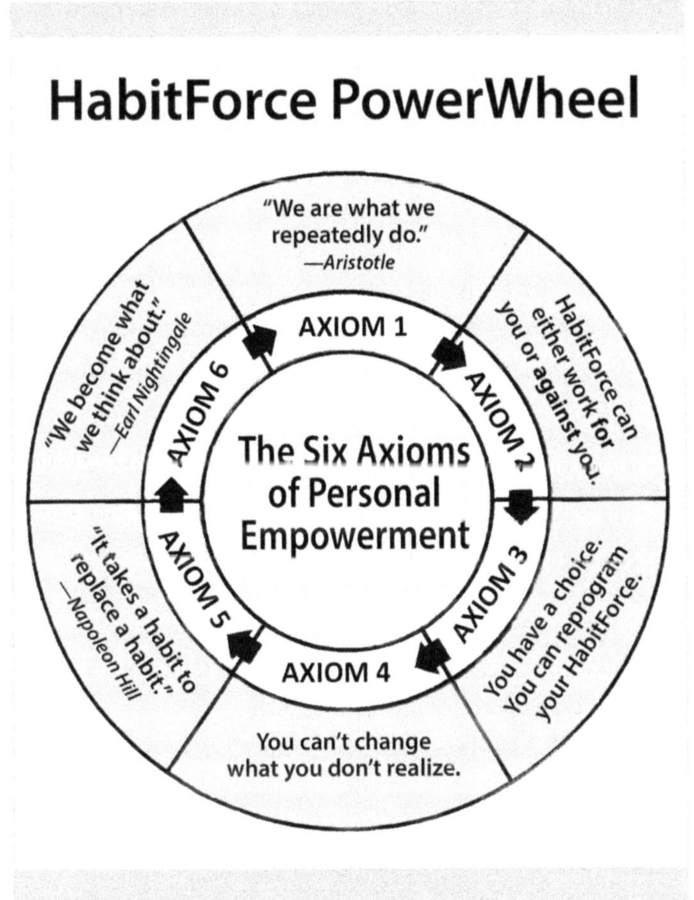

The HabitForce PowerWheel: The Six Axioms of Personal Empowerment

MAKE A HABIT OF KEEPING PROMISES

In a very real sense, the book I promised my mother I would finish writing is both a prequel and an essential companion for this book about the power of promises. In *HabitForce! How to Kick the Habits of FAILURE and Adopt the Habits of SUCCESS*, I introduce the seven disempowering failure traps that hold people back from reaching their goals and keeping their promises. For every one of these failure habits there is an equal-but-opposite habit of success. The book features two side-by-side, seven-letter acronyms – FAILURE and SUCCESS – with each letter standing for a particular habit of failure or success.

I'd like to briefly summarize two critical SUCCESS habits that I believe are most closely related to changing your life and keeping your promises. All seven SUCCESS habits are important, of course, but I regard the two I outline below as being directly related to the ongoing, habitual process of changing your life and keeping your promises.

SUCCESS HABIT #1: SHOULDER RESPONSIBILITY

This success habit is fundamental to personal change. If you fail to take responsibility for all aspects of your life, you simply can't make meaningful changes. The corresponding FAILURE habit is "Finger Pointing," making excuses or playing the blame game. If you find yourself Finger Pointing on a regular basis, you need to stop and develop the habit of taking or shouldering responsibility for your life. Unlike finger-pointers, the person who shoulders responsibility doesn't waste time or energy looking for someone or something to blame.

There's nothing more powerful and personally empowering than the moment when you accept the fact that you are in control of your own life. If you're going to point fingers, be sure the finger is pointed at yourself. That's when you start to take personal responsibility for your successes and failures.

Then, and only then, can you reliably make promises and keep them. Then, and only then, will you be able to make positive changes in your life.

"The person who is good at making excuses is seldom good at anything else."
— Benjamin Franklin

In *The 7 Habits of Highly Effective People*, Stephen Covey writes about a person's "Circle of Concern" and "Circle of Influence." Covey points out that ineffective people fret over and put energy into things that they can't control – these things become their Circle of Concern – such as the actions of others and negative events that happened in the past. Effective people, by contrast, focus their attention on things that they can do something about – their Circle of Influence – such as their career paths, the time they set aside for their families, solutions to problems, enhancing their job skills, exercising, improving their diet, and finding a better job.

If you find yourself dwelling on the past – a common characteristic of finger-pointers – remind yourself that you can't change the past, but you can certainly deal with the present. And you can strive to make the future better. One of the most fundamental keys to success is to spend time and energy working on the things you can do something about... right now.

Shouldering responsibility also implies – indeed requires – a high standard of personal ethics. Honesty, integrity, and accountability are essential qualities that support taking responsibility. It's important to establish a habit of simple honesty, both in your internal dialogue and in your dealings with others.

Habitual dishonesty, mendacity, outright lying, lack of integrity are all part and parcel of the finger-pointing mentality with its emphasis on shifting blame instead of accepting accountability. You simply can't become the master of your own destiny if you habitually live in a make-believe world built on a flimsy foundation of falsehoods.

The old cliché is true: Honesty is the best policy. In fact, it is the only policy if you want to shoulder responsibility for your life. That's key to keeping your promises and changing your life.

AFFIRMATION: SHOULDER RESPONSIBILITY

To create and sustain the habit of shouldering responsibility, I suggest that you repeat the following short affirmation to yourself several times a day. You may draft your own affirmation but be sure to state it in the present tense and keep it positive. Reinforce the behavior you seek to affirm as if it is already reality.

I willingly and eagerly shoulder responsibility for my life. I'm in charge of what I do and my reactions to what happens to me. I'm in the driver's seat of my life, my hands are firmly on the steering wheel and I freely choose the direction my life takes. I recognize that this is crucial if I want to keep my promises and change my life.

KEEP A PERSONAL DIARY

I also recommend that you keep a personal diary or notebook so you can keep track of the times you catch yourself finger-pointing. Listen especially to that inner voice that keeps chattering away like an irritating play-by-play sports announcer who just won't shut up. Notice any finger-pointing patterns. Do you have a familiar list of excuses? Write them down. Also, write down examples of when you succeed in shouldering responsibility for what happens in your life. This is key to turning things around and making important changes in your life.

SUCCESS HABIT #2: SET YOUR COURSE

We've already covered the benefits of turning important goals into heartfelt promises. So, I won't delve into this habit in too much detail. I simply want to underscore for you here how crucial it is to know where you're going. You should want to blaze a trail toward a definite destination, with a clear goal that you pursue with a burning desire.

That's essentially what a promise can do for you. It sets your course toward a specific and heartfelt goal. And if you can make a habit of setting your course with the help of a few heartfelt promises, you'll be in an ideal position to succeed in making positive changes in your life.

I've heard the word "goal" defined as a dream with a deadline. I like that. Setting your course is all about fulfilling your dreams. But you need goals – dreams with deadlines – to get there. You need to set your course and take positive steps toward your ultimate goals in life.

The first step in setting your course is to write your personal mission statement. This helps you establish a clear purpose, set long-term goals, and begin mapping out plans to reach your destination. Here's a hint: Your mission statement should link directly to what you're passionate about, a career or direction in life that truly excites you.

Briefly described, the corresponding FAILURE habit is what I refer to as Reactive Mindset. This habit is devoid of purpose. This is the habit of drifting, of being bounced around like a pinball by events, circumstances, and the desires of other people. It's the mindset that never plans.

Once you get in the habit of setting your course – once you know where you want to go – you're able to break away from the gravitational pull of negative, aimless, purposeless drift. With a clear purpose in mind, backed by a powerful promise, you're empowered. Knowing where you want to go reinforces other successful habits, like Shouldering Responsibility. You naturally shoulder responsibility because you recognize that you're on a path of your own choosing.

A great way to stay on a positive track is to think about your legacy. When all is said and done, what kind of legacy will you leave behind? What will others – especially your loved ones – say and think about you and what you have achieved. In *Harness Your HabitForce* and my HabitForce programs, I talk about The Ebenezer Effect, named after Ebenezer Scrooge in Dickens' *A Christmas Carol.* I gave it that name because Scrooge visits his gravestone and learns what people think of him after he's gone when he is transported into the future by the ghost of Christmas yet to come. I won't recount all the details here. Suffice it to say, you can set your course by writing your own eulogy. Take stock of your life's accomplishments – or what you hope they will be. That's The Ebenezer Effect in a nutshell. It's a sobering thought to consider your own mortality, but it does help to focus the mind on the most important things in life. On things like your purpose and your legacy. You can harness The Ebenezer Effect by promising to write your own eulogy. It's a powerful mission statement for your life.

AFFIRMATION: SET YOUR COURSE

To make lasting changes in your life, you must begin by going inward, through meditation and quiet reflection, and asking yourself a key question: What is your purpose in life? Trust in your ability to identify your purpose. Not having a mission or purpose is part of the Reactive Mindset FAILURE trap. Identifying your purpose is the way out.

I suggest that you repeat the following short affirmation to yourself several times a day. You may draft your own affirmation but be sure to state it in the present tense and keep it positive. Reinforce the behavior you seek to affirm as if it is already reality.

I know my mission in life, and I set my course
in the direction of my goals and dreams.
I turn important goals into heartfelt promises.
I happily map out my destination because knowing
where I'm going empowers me and allows me to
persevere despite setbacks and distractions.

PERSONAL DIARY

Write down ideas about your mission in life, your purpose. Meditate on the question: What is my purpose in life? Notice how you spend your time. Are your activities leading you in the direction of your life's purpose? Are you simply reacting to events and circumstances or people as they appear? What's your long term goal and how can you begin to make progress toward it? Write a mission statement for your life that captures those things that are most important to you and points you in the direction of achieving long-term goals and fulfilling your life's purpose.

Personal Empowerment Promises – PEPTalks
A Promise a Day: 30 Days to a Promising Future
Top 10 Promises for a SUCCESSFUL Life

To stay on track over time, to counter the natural tendency backslide, you must routinely give yourself internal pep talks through positive self-talk, affirmations, and optimistic thoughts and expectations. We all need a good pep talk now and then, especially when we're feeling under the weather or a little low on energy or motivation. It happens to the best of us.

Webster's dictionary defines pep talk as "a vigorous, emotional talk intended to inspire enthusiasm, increase determination to succeed." The term derives from pep (short for "pepper") and means "lively spirits or energy; vigor; animation."

To help you stay motivated and moving toward your promises and your purpose, I created "A Promise a Day: 30 Days to a Promising Future." It involves a daily practice of writing down and repeating what I call "Personal Empowerment Promises" (PEPs). The tagline for this program is: A pep talk in every promise!

The notion that people can use the power of making a promise as a personal empowerment tool – an idea that I think isn't widely appreciated or employed – is embraced by a global organization called Optimist International. This association of more than 2,900 Optimist Clubs around the world is dedicated to "Bringing Out the Best in Kids."

Optimist International is best known for what has become known as "The Optimist Creed" by Christian D. Larson. A version of this well-known classic of positive thinking first appeared in Larson's 1912 book *Your Forces and How to Use Them*. Not known as "The Optimist Creed" at that time, it appeared in the first chapter of Larson's book under the heading "Promise Yourself." Optimist International adopted "Promise Yourself" as The Optimist Creed in 1922.

The Optimist Creed boils down to a collection of what I have dubbed "Personal Empowerment Promises" (PEPs). A slightly abridged version of Larson's inspiring words appears today on Optimist International's website.

Inspired by these remarkable Personal Empowerment Promises in "The Optimist Creed," I originally launched my "A Promise A Day: 30 Days to a Promising Future" program as a series of short daily tweets on Twitter/X (@MakeAPromiseDay). These promises provide you with positive, inspiring, optimistic "thought bursts" to keep you on track and moving in the right direction.

To gain maximum benefit from this program, I encourage you to:

- Start your day by reading that day's promise thoughtfully, considering the promise as a whole and key words. Don't just think about the promise but get a real feel for it – what it means to you and how it resonates with you. If you'd like to personalize any of the suggested promises, go ahead and change a few words, but aim to retain the main message.
- Write down each day's promise, perhaps in your Promise Journal at least 10 times, either first thing in the morning or over the course of a day. Don't write the promise hurriedly. Take your time. Let every word "sink in."
- Further reinforce each day's promise by repeating it aloud or silently to yourself several times over the course of the day. Don't be surprised if the promise

suddenly pops into your mind – it's becoming part of your self-talk.

When you've gone through the entire 30-day program … go through it again! There's no limit to the benefits of giving yourself personal empowerment messages.

Or, if you prefer, create an abbreviated version of the program. I suggest that you use the "Top 10" promises (Days 20-29) that form the acronym SUCCESSFUL as a core group, and then select a few additional promises from the 30-day program that resonate most strongly with you. You might even want to create and incorporate a few promises of your own. For best results, they should be short, easily remembered "thought bursts" that encapsulate positive, affirmative ideas and feelings.

Go through this collection of promises as you did with the full program, several times a day writing down that day's promise and repeating it to yourself aloud or silently to yourself.

Tuning into your Personal Empowerment Promises every day is key to ingraining these promises into your memory and etching them onto your subconscious mind. Always remember: The most powerful motivational speech in the world is what you say to yourself! And not just occasionally but repeatedly, habitually. Your habitual internal dialogue, your perpetual self-talk, will determine your destiny.

A Promise a Day: 30 Days to a Promising Future, including the Top 10 Promises for a SUCCESSFUL Life

Day 1: Personal Empowerment Promise #1

Adapted from Christian D. Larson

I PROMISE to forget the mistakes of the past and press on to the greater achievements of the future.

Day 2: Personal Empowerment Promise #2

Adapted from Christian D. Larson

I PROMISE to talk health, happiness, and prosperity to every person I meet.

Day 3: Personal Empowerment Promise #3

I PROMISE to savor every moment of life, appreciating that time is my most precious, non-renewable resource.

Day 4: Personal Empowerment Promise #4

Adapted from a quote often attributed to Mahatma Gandhi

I PROMISE to be the change I want to see in the world

Day 5: Personal Empowerment Promise #5

I PROMISE to think only of the best, to work only for the best, and to expect only the best.

Day 6: Personal Empowerment Promise #6

I PROMISE to follow the Golden Rule and always treat others as I want to be treated myself.

Day 7: Personal Empowerment Promise #7

Adapted from Christian D. Larson

I PROMISE to give so much time to improving myself that I have no time to criticize others.

Day 8: Personal Empowerment Promise #8

Adapted from Christian D. Larson

I PROMISE to be just as enthusiastic about the success of others as I am about my own.

Day 9: Personal Empowerment Promise #9

I PROMISE to embrace a healthy lifestyle that includes proper diet, exercise, moderation and balance and avoids harmful addictions.

Day 10: Personal Empowerment Promise #10

Adapted from Christian D. Larson

I PROMISE to be so strong that nothing can disturb my peace of mind.

Day 11: Personal Empowerment Promise #11

Adapted from Christian D. Larson

I PROMISE to focus my thoughts and attention on what I want in my life, not on what I don't want, because what we focus on expands.

Day 12: Personal Empowerment Promise #12

Adapted from Christian D. Larson

I PROMISE to make all my friends feel that there is something worthwhile in them.

Day 13: Personal Empowerment Promise #13

I PROMISE to be too large for worry, too noble for anger, too strong for fear, and too happy to permit the presence of trouble.

Day 14: Personal Empowerment Promise #14

Adapted from Christian D. Larson

I PROMISE to look at the sunny side of everything and make my optimism come true.

Day 15: Personal Empowerment Promise #15

I PROMISE to recognize that my present thoughts will determine my future reality because what we think is what we get.

Day 16: Personal Empowerment Promise #16

Adapted from Christian D. Larson

I PROMISE to wear a cheerful expression at all times and give a smile to every living creature I meet.

Day 17: Personal Empowerment Promise #17

I PROMISE to get started and keep going, learning from my mistakes and from those who tried and failed many times but didn't give up.

Day 18: Personal Empowerment Promise #18

Adapted from Christian D. Larson

I PROMISE to think well of myself and to proclaim this fact to the world, not in loud words, but in great deeds.

Day 19: Personal Empowerment Promise #19

Adapted from Christian D. Larson

I PROMISE to live in the faith that the whole world is on my side, so long as I am true to the best that is in me.

[Author's Note: For the next 10 Personal Empowerment Promises, the letters that begin each promise form the acronym SUCCESSFUL and constitute "The Top 10 Promises for a SUCCESSFUL Life."

Day 20: Personal Empowerment Promise #20

S I PROMISE to **Shoulder Responsibility** for my life and destiny, placing myself behind the wheel, in charge with no excuses.

Day 21: Personal Empowerment Promise #21

U I PROMISE to **Unite with Eagles** by associating with positive role models of personal achievement, integrity and service.

Day 22: Personal Empowerment Promise #22

C I PROMISE to **Carpe Diem** – Seize the Day – regularly taking action and seizing opportunities to achieve my goals, dreams, purpose … and keep my promises.

Day 23: Personal Empowerment Promise #23

C I PROMISE to **Cultivate Enthusiasm**, purpose and happiness in my life by discovering, embracing and pursuing my true passions. Life is not a dress rehearsal!

Day 24: Personal Empowerment Promise #24

E I PROMISE to **Empower Myself** by harnessing my HabitForce and by continuous self-improvement to reach my peak potential in life.

Day 25: Personal Empowerment Promise #25

S I PROMISE to **Set My Course** in alignment with my Dharma, my purpose, my passion, and toward my dreams, goals and promises.

Day 26: Personal Empowerment Promise #26

S I PROMISE to **Sow Optimism and Joy** in my life and the lives of others, recognizing that happiness is the ultimate success.

Day 27: Personal Empowerment Promise #27

F I PROMISE to **Focus on Financial Freedom**, purposefully receiving abundance for myself and generously helping others do the same.

Day 28: Personal Empowerment Promise #28

U I PROMISE to **Unleash the Power of Gratitude** by counting my blessings and appreciating daily the many things I'm grateful for.

Day 29: Personal Empowerment Promise #29

L I PROMISE to **Love** … to love my life, to genuinely feel and express love, and to consciously create a lasting legacy of love.

Day 30: Personal Empowerment Promise #30

I PROMISE to keep my promises… and to help others keep theirs.

"Be the change you want to see in the world."
- often attributed to Mahatma Gandhi

CHAPTER 7

Transform the World: An Invitation and a Challenge

Congratulations! You are about to be powered up by the all-important fourth booster rocket: Transform the World. Here's a reminder of the four-part structure we've been following:

Make a Promise.
Keep Your Word.
Change Your Life.
TRANSFORM THE WORLD

You're probably aware of a famous Robert Frost poem ("Stopping by Woods on a Snowy Evening.") that ends with these memorable, oft-quoted lines:

The woods are lovely, dark and deep,
But I have promises to keep,
And miles to go before I sleep,
And miles to go before I sleep.

In the preceding pages, you've learned about the promise I made to my mother that launched me on a quest to share the power of a promise. You've read about how promises can help you Believe More, Achieve More, and Receive More. You've encountered those two magic words – "I promise" – numerous times. And you've read that promises come from the heart and are backed with strong emotion. You've also learned that a promise is like a goal on steroids and that you should follow the G.P.S. Success Formula: From Goals to Promises = Success.

You've read inspiring stories about promises made and promises kept. You've seen how lives, communities, and even the course of history can be changed by promises. A terrific example of changing the course of history – one that is close to my heart as a former NATO speechwriter – is the promise made by members of NATO to come to the defense of their fellow members. This mutual-defense promise has helped to keep the peace in Europe since 1949.

In this chapter, I will expand upon the "Transforming the World" potential of promises, about taking the power of a promise "on the road," so to speak, sharing it with others, spreading the word, joining a movement to transform the world through the power of promises, one person and one promise at a time. I invite you – and I challenge you – to join me in this transformational mission.

The promise I made to my mother changed my life. I had a sudden epiphany – upon rereading the dedication to my book *HabitForce!* – that there was something uniquely powerful about promises in the human experience. The more I explored this idea, the more enthused I became about my mission is to share the power of promises with millions of people around the world.

I have told many people about this exciting mission, among them John Assaraf, who offered these kind and supportive words:

"I have spoken with Matthew about his project related to the Power of Making a Promise. He told me about 'Make A Promise Day' and his mission to highlight what he calls those

two magic words: 'I Promise.' I agree completely .... There is something uniquely powerful about making a promise that goes beyond traditional goal setting. I was delighted to share a personal story with Matthew about a very special promise I made in my own life. I believe Matthew's mission has the potential to be of enormous benefit to many others and I offer him my very best wishes for success in compiling these uplifting stories about promises made and promises kept. Put simply, Matthew's project is very promising indeed!"

TAKING MY PERSONAL MISSION PUBLIC

A few years ago, I turned my mission into a public promise. I first made this rather audacious promise as a guest on Norm Lapalme's "Million Dollar Idea" radio show based in Ottawa, Canada.

I first met Norm at a success seminar hosted by my friend, bestselling author and speaker Peggy McColl. Norm, a remarkably gifted, insightful entrepreneur and coach, was one of the scheduled speakers. The day before his scheduled session, I had the pleasure of speaking extensively with Norm about the promise I made to my mother and my plans to write a book about the power of making a promise.

To my surprise, when Norm took the stage the next day, he announced to the hundreds of attendees: "I spoke with Matthew Cossolotto yesterday about the promise he made to his mother and his 'Power of Making a Promise' concept. I believe this truly is a million-dollar idea."

Norm consulted with me about my power-of-making-a-promise idea for several months and then invited me to be a guest on his radio program. During his interview with me, I spoke about my "Take the Promise Challenge" concept of turning an important goal into a heartfelt promise ... and watching the magic happen. Quite deftly, Norm immediately challenged me to make a public promise on his program. I promised that I would turn "Make A Promise Day" on May 4th and the power of making a promise into a major initiative that will be recognized by, and positively affect the lives of, millions of people around the world.

I have repeated this promise to many people on many occasions. I have done so because I firmly believe that sharing a promise with others energizes the promise and makes it more powerful. I also believe that in making promises public, together we can transform the world, one person and one promise at a time.

I continue to work on this promise. But I can't do it alone. Writing and publicizing this book are important steps in the process of world transformation. This book is one way for me to begin to fulfill my promise. But I'm going to need lots of help from lots of wonderful people to keep this audacious promise. More specifically, I'm going to need YOUR help. I hope readers of this book will feel a sense of ownership about the power of promises to change lives and that you'll feel moved to join with me in launching and promoting a worldwide "Make a Promise" movement.

This chapter describes several ideas and initiatives for spreading the word about the power of making a promise, including "Make A Promise Day" on May 4th and outlines specific steps you can take to play a part in this important effort.

You should know that this book is only one step – and important step – in this process. I foresee additional promise-related books featuring inspirational stories about life-changing promises made and promises kept. I hope you will support additional books in this series by reading them and spreading the word to friends, relatives and associates.

You can also help by sending me your own inspiring promise stories. If you'd like to share your promise story with me for possible inclusion in future books in this series or in my workshops and other programs, please see instructions for submitting promise stories and ideas in the "Resources" section at the back of this book. These stories could be about promises made by students, teachers, parents, couples, children, grandparents, corporations, or political, civic and religious leaders, even celebrities.

You could also send me any promise stories you've read or heard about that involve a famous contemporary or historical figure. I strongly suspect that just about any biography or autobiography of any noteworthy person will include, somewhere, the story of a promise made, and a promise kept. The same is true, I believe, of just about any memorable and lasting work of literature. So, if you come across uplifting stories about promises made and kept – in real life or from literature, films or television – please share them with me for possible inclusion in future books in this series or in my interviews and presentations. Your support is very much appreciated.

Komen for the Cure: Nancy Brinker's Promise to Her Sister

"I promise, Suzy … even if it takes the rest of my life."

This powerful promise comes from Ambassador Nancy Brinker, a recognized leader in the global movement to find a cure for breast cancer. Her journey began with a simple promise to her dying sister, Susan G. Komen, that she would do everything possible to create awareness and help find a cure for breast cancer, which took Susan's life at a young age. Brinker also wants to end the shame, pain, fear and hopelessness caused by this terrible disease. In one generation, the organization that bears Susan's name, has changed the world.

Brinker tells the story of her promise to her sister in a moving book titled, *Promise Me: How a Sister's Love Launched the Global Movement to End Breast Cancer.* The following comments about Brinker's book from former First Lady Laura Bush underscore the unique power of making a promise:

"Nancy's love for her cherished sister sparked a promise to fight breast cancer. Today that promise has launched a global movement to end breast cancer, and Nancy is fulfilling her promise to women all around the world."

Brinker's efforts to battle breast cancer were honored by President Barack Obama in 2009. He awarded her the Presidential Medal of Freedom, the nation's highest civilian honor. Also in 2009, the United Nation's World Health Organization named her Goodwill Ambassador for Cancer Control.

CREATING NEW PROMISE TRADITIONS

Here's another way to help. I hope you'll embrace this idea and share it with friends and relatives. To inject even more emotional meaning to the promises we make, I believe we should consider adopting several new promise-related traditions. One way to do this is to establish a special day dedicated to making promises. That's why I created "Make A Promise Day" on May 4. (See discussion below.)

We could also inject additional emotion into our promises by making promises on existing holidays and other occasions that hold special meaning for us. Doing so will help to anchor your promise emotionally by linking it with special days in the year.

For example, on Father's Day in 2010, Kirk Smalley made a promise to do everything possible to put an end to bullying after his 11-year-old stepson, Ty Field, committed suicide. Ty took his life after being suspended from school when he retaliated against a student who had been bullying him for over two years.

Kirk's promise has propelled him, along with his wife and Ty's mother Laura, to visit more than a thousand schools and speak to more than a million students to raise awareness about bullying and the devastation it can cause. In March 2012, Kirk and Laura met privately with President Barack Obama and First Lady Michelle Obama in the White House prior to participating in the first-ever White House conference on bullying.

The fact that Kirk Smalley decided to make this promise on Father's Day adds a great deal of poignancy to a day in the year that already holds special meaning for fathers and their children.

In this spirit, I think we should consider the following:

- Make a promise on birthdays – our own and other peoples' birthdays. This would require a very simple amendment to the traditions we already celebrate on birthdays. We often light birthday candles, and the person celebrating a birthday makes a wish and then blows out the candles. Why not make a public promise and blow out the candles? What's more powerful a promise or a wish? These aren't mutually exclusive by any means. You could do both – make a public promise and a private wish. Birthday celebrations offer a terrific opportunity to make our promises public since we're often surrounded by family and friends on our birthdays. We could also use the celebrations on the birthday of a friend or loved one to make a public promise to that person. Likewise, we could use the birthday of a special person in history or in your family to make a promise. Doing so will serve to increase your emotional commitment to the promise.

- Make a promise on Mother's Day. This is a perfect time to make a promise to your mother. Give her flowers *and* a promise. Young people, for example, could promise their mothers that they won't drink and drive, and that they'll make sure that their brothers, sisters and friends won't either. Mother's Day could also be an occasion for mothers to make promises to their children, families, communities — to just about anybody about just about anything because, after all, it's their special day and it's bursting with promise.
- Make a promise on Father's Day. All my suggestions for Mother's Day apply equally to Father's Day. Because these days are already charged with emotion, making a promise on these special days will put a little bit more of a charge behind your promise.
- Make a Patriotic Promise (to vote or serve the country in some capacity) on Independence Day (July 4th in the United States) or another national holiday in other countries. In other countries, you could make a promise on some special national day. In the U.S., perhaps

it's time for millions of citizens to make a promise to strengthen our democracy through pro-democracy reforms related to improving our voting system or creating a national election-day holiday. Voting on the traditional Tuesday election day – typically a workday for most Americans – is inconvenient at best and sometimes virtually impossible. Early voting and vote-by-mail alternatives have helped to make voting more accessible. But I think we should make voting even easier for our fellow citizens by making voter registration automatic and election day a National Holiday. Doing so will send a strong signal to citizens that we put a high value on voting.

- Make a romantic promise to that special someone on Valentine's Day.
- Make a special promise at a wedding (as part of a toast) or at a funeral (as part of a eulogy).
- Make a promise to your spouse on your wedding anniversary. Or invite your spouse to make a promise to you!
- Parents can make a promise to their child on Graduation Day. And their son and daughter graduates can make a promise to their parents.
- Make a promise to take care of newborn children. (See John Assaraf's promise.)
- Turn one or more of your New Year's Resolutions into New Year's Promises.
- Select other days of the year that have special meaning to you – like a parent's or a child's birthday – and make a few heartfelt promises on those specific days.

The options are virtually endless, and the results in terms of personal empowerment, goal achievement and integrity enhancement could be priceless. The point is to increase your level of emotional commitment by making a heartfelt promise and anchoring the promise to a special event or existing holiday. You're much more likely to keep your word.

Dr. Raul Ruiz's Promise to His Community

Raul Ruiz, the son of migrant farm workers in Coachella Valley, California, wanted to be a doctor, but there was no money for college or medical school. Nearly two-thirds of migrant farm workers, for all their back-breaking labor, have a median income of less than $7,500 a year, well below the poverty line.

After graduating from high school in 2001, Ruiz went door-to-door to business owners in his community and made a promise: If they would contribute to his education, he would return to practice medicine in Coachella Valley, which was in dire need of doctors. He gave a handwritten, signed promise contract to every person who contributed. His community rallied behind the determined young man, providing enough funds for him to complete a bachelor's degree at the University of California Los Angeles – he spent his summer breaks back home, volunteering at the farm workers' medical clinic – and then a medical degree and two master's degrees from Harvard.

Just as he had promised, the Ruiz returned home to practice medicine, working in the Emergency Department at Eisenhower Medical Center. He also helped open a free clinic for underserved residents and helped start a mentorship program for students who want to become doctors, among many other initiatives.

In 2012, Ruiz ran for election to the U.S. House of Representatives to have an even greater positive impact. "I want to fix the problems and improve the lives of the people I serve," Ruiz stated. During is congressional career, he has emphasized improving the quality and accessibility of health care for the more than 700,000 people of California's 25th Congressional District.

CREATE A PROMISE COMMUNITY

I hope you'll sign up to be part of our growing Promise Community. Through online communications and local gatherings, we'll be able to explore ways to spread the word about the power of promises, about keeping our own promises and encouraging others to keep theirs. Having virtual and real-world support groups will allow promise-makers to make their promises public and to discuss the progress and the difficulties they've experienced in keeping their promises. Promise Circles or Promise Networks could also form the nucleus of people who support adoption of "Make-A-Promise Day" Proclamations in their local communities.

To transform the world, we'll need to establish and nurture a growing community of people who make a habit of turning important goals into heartfelt promises. I hope you'll foster the growth of a worldwide promise community, one that can bridge national, cultural, ethnic and religious differences. To help make this happen, I urge leaders in local, city, state, national jurisdictions around the world to adopt "Make A Promise Day" proclamations.

MAKE A PROMISE DAY, MAY 4

Which brings me to my initiative called "Make A Promise Day." This is an annual celebration of the power of promises that occurs on May 4th. I launched the very first Make A Promise Day on May 4, 2010. It was the opening salvo in my campaign to spread the word about the power of a promise. "Make A Promise Day" is one day that I hope millions of people around the world will coalesce around as a day they select to turn a couple of important goals into heartfelt promises.

Make A Promise Day (MAPD for short) is an unofficial "holiday" dedicated to personal empowerment, goal achievement and integrity enhancement. Make A Promise Day speaks to a key message of this book: That the solution to our problems, and the problems of the world, isn't "out there" somewhere, but is "in here," inside each one of us.

MAPD is a key part of my ongoing mission to share the power of making a promise with millions of people around the world. As a guest on Norm Lapalme's "Million Dollar Idea" radio program, I made a public promise to turn "Make A Promise Day" into a widely recognized "holiday" around the world.

There are lots of special days each year, some of which are official holidays. Some aren't holidays but they carry important emotional weight – Mother's Day or Father's Day, for instance. Or Valentine's Day. I thought MAPD might become one of those special days that people celebrate because they resonate emotionally with the purpose behind the day.

Since Make A Promise Day is all about helping people empower themselves by turning important goals into heartfelt promises and by making and keeping those promises, I wanted to select a day on the calendar that conveyed this message of personal empowerment. Once again, an epiphany hit me: "Make A Promise Day" had to be on May 4th. Because then I could say the following sentence and it would make sense: May the Fourth be with you!

I know it's a silly pun, but people get it. And importantly, they don't *forget* it. "May the Fourth be with you" is memorable. Personal change and transforming the world doesn't have to be boring. It can be fun.

I also know that some people think of May 4th as Star Wars Day because the phrase "May the Force be with you" originated in that movie franchise. But when I first thought of Make a Promise Day – May the Fourth be with you – I had no idea May 4th was known by some as Star Wars Day. I only heard about the coincidence several years later.

There's no reason Make a Promise Day and Star Wars Day can't co-exist on the same day. Besides, I could make the argument that the power of a promise is exactly the kind of positive, life-affirming "force" that can make a real difference in the world. Surely, sharing May 4th with Make a Promise Day will not cause a disturbance in the Force.

Here's what my friend, public relations guru, author and entrepreneur Rick Frishman said about "Make A Promise Day."

"Happy 'Make A Promise Day' everybody! I really like Matthew's idea. The power of making a promise to someone you care about really can change your life. Great work Matthew ... May The Fourth Be With You!"

Brian Proctor, publisher of Insight of the Day, sent this message to tens of thousands of his subscribers:

"I want to call your attention to an exciting and inspiring initiative created by my friend Matthew Cossolotto. Matthew's project launched last year on this day. He calls it "Make A Promise Day" – the first-ever "holiday" dedicated to personal empowerment and goal achievement. With "Make A Promise Day," Matthew is encouraging people to turn important goals into heartfelt promises. I really like that idea and I thought it would appeal to you as well."

And I thank TV host and life coach Todd Newton for sharing his promise story with me and for the following words of encouragement:

"I look forward to supporting your "Make A Promise Day" in May and being part of this great campaign as it grows, and grows, and grows."

IDEAS FOR "MAKE A PROMISE DAY" PROMISES

In case you're looking for inspiration for the kinds of promises you could make on "Make A Promise Day," check out the following suggestions given to me by a couple of friends:

My friend, Diane DiResta (www.Diresta.com), urged readers of her blog to make a promise to become a better public speaker. As we all know, public speaking is a key leadership and success skill. So, Diane – author, speaking strategist, professional speaker, and consultant – suggested that people should use the occasion of "Make A Promise Day" to make a promise to achieve this goal. Here's how Diane described this:

"Why make a promise? Because a promise is more powerful than a goal. Quick! How many New Year's Resolutions have you already broken? When you promise to be a better public speaker, there is an energy and commitment that drives you to action. My military father taught me to never break a promise. When you gave someone your word, that was sacred … A promise is putting a stake in the ground. It's drawing a line in the sand. You can become a better public speaker right now and the first step begins with a promise."

Another suggestion for a "Make A Promise Day" promise comes from my friend Andrea Adams-Miller (https://igniteyourrelationship.com/). Andrea is a keynote speaker, interpersonal relationship consultant, business consultant, author, columnist, and an award-winning talk radio show host. In a blog post, she recommended that you make a promise to foster a healthy relationship. In Andrea's words:

"This blog is inspired by my friend, Matthew Cossolotto, creator of "Make A Promise Day" because I would like all of you to make a promise to your partner. While Matthew discusses various financial, moral, and personal decisions when it comes to making a promise, my challenge to you is focused on your relationship and your partner. As a relationship con-

sultant, I want you to make a promise to keep the words "Break Up" and "Divorce" out of your vocabulary. Each time we utter these words, we add power to them and start imaging our life as somehow happier if we were alone, rather than deal with the day-to-day stresses of maintaining a healthy relationship."

Keep in mind that you can make any promise you want on "Make A Promise Day." You might select a promise from the Personal Empowerment Promises contained in Chapter 6 or make a heartfelt promise all your own.

MY "MAKE A PROMISE DAY" PROMISE

As mentioned, I have made several public promises that I will turn "Make A Promise Day" into a widely recognized day for celebrating the power of making a promise around the world. The first time I made such a promise was during my guest appearance on Norm Lapalme's "Million Dollar Idea" radio show. But I have also made this same promise on other radio shows and, specifically, on "Make A Promise Day" itself. In fact, every "Make A Promise Day" I include this promise in my short list of public promises.

I'm pleased to say that "Make A Promise Day" has become an officially recognized day in both the town of Yorktown Heights, New York, and in Westchester County, New York.

Here is a model Make a Promise Day Proclamation that you could adapt for local, state, provincial, national, or international jurisdictions:

Office of ______________________

____

(Insert Town, City, County, State/Province, Country or Organization)

Make a PROMISE Day

May 4th

May The Fourth Be With You!

Contact: Matthew Cossolotto, www.MakeAPromiseDay.com

PROCLAMATION

WHEREAS: MAKE A PROMISE DAY IS THE ONLY UNOFFICIAL "HOLIDAY" DEDICATED TO PERSONAL EMPOWERMENT, GOAL ACHIEVEMENT AND INTEGRITY ENHANCEMENT, AND;

WHEREAS: MAKE A PROMISE DAY ENCOURAGES INDIVIDUALS TO TURN IMPORTANT GOALS INTO HEARTFELT PROMISES, THEREBY INCREASING THE PROBABILITY OF REACHING THOSE GOALS, AND;

WHEREAS: CELEBRATING MAKE A PROMISE DAY WILL HAVE THE EFFECT OF ENHANCING ACCOUNTABILITY, PERSONAL RESPONSIBILITY AND INTEGRITY, AND;

THE (INSERT TITLE ______________________) RECOGNIZES THE VALUE OF HIGHLIGHTING THE POWER OF MAKING AND KEEPING PROMISES ON THE PART OF LOCAL STUDENTS, TEACHERS, COMMUNITY ORGANIZATIONS, BUSINESSES AND POLITICAL LEADERS;

NOW, THEREFORE, I, (NAME AND TITLE ______________________), DO HEREBY PROCLAIM MAY 4, (INSERT YEAR ______) AND EACH YEAR THEREAFTER TO BE MAKE A PROMISE DAY AND ENCOURAGE ORGANIZATIONS AND INDIVIDUAL MEMBERS OF THE COMMUNITY TO CELEBRATE THIS VERY IMPORTANT DAY IN A MANNER THEY DEEM TO BE SUITABLE AND APPROPRIATE.

(SIGNED ______________________) (DATE ______________________)

PROMISES TO KEEP: TRANSFORM THE WORLD!

This official recognition of "Make A Promise Day" is only a start. With your help, I would like to spread the word far and wide – through this book, media interviews and my guest speaking programs. Please share this proclamation with officials in your town, city, state/province, or nation and encourage them to issue the "Make A Promise Day" proclamation. There are no costs involved. But there are many benefits that will accrue to any jurisdiction that openly encourages citizens to tap into the power of making a promise.

As I hope I've made clear in these pages, my interest in promoting "Make A Promise Day" and the power of making a promise more generally goes beyond helping people change their lives for the better. That's a big part of it. But I'm also interested in transforming the world. Making the world a better place. It may take a village to raise a child, but it takes a promise – many individual promises – to transform the world.

I'll remind you again about Matthew's Mantra. This sums up what the power of making a promise is all about:

Make a Promise.
Keep Your Word.
Change Your Life.
Transform the World.

Holocaust Survivor Sonia Schreiber Weitz's Promise That She Would Tell the World

Sonia Schreiber Weitz employed the power of a promise to make a big difference in the world. Through poetry and testimony in her book, *I Promised I Would Tell*, Sonia Weitz kept her word that she would tell the world about what happened to her and millions of others during the Holocaust.

When Sonia was 11 years old, she was relocated from her home in Krakow, Poland, to a Nazi concentration camp. Over the next five years, she survived the horrors of five different death camps: Plaszow, Auschwitz, Bergen-Belsen, Venusberg, and Mauthausen. At 16, Sonia was liberated from Mauthausen. She weighed only 60 pounds and was suffering from typhus. An American soldier found her near death lying in a bunk. He gathered her in his arms and carried her to freedom.

Sonia's mother and more than 80 members of her extended family perished in the Holocaust. Only Sonia and her older sister, Blanca, survived. When Sonia's mother was taken to away from Sonia, her last words to Sonia were: "Promise that you will tell. Promise me you won't forget."

Sonia promised her mother. Years later she told the *Boston Globe* that the task of remembering the untold suffering of those years was almost unbearable. In another interview, she asked: "How does one bear witness to the unspeakable?"

Somehow, she found the courage and the right words. Having made the promise to her mother, she was determined to tell the world what had happened. During her years in concentration camps, Sonia was not allowed to have a pencil or paper. She had to memorize the poems she composed during her early teen years spent in inhuman confinement.

After her liberation in 1945, Sonia and her sister made their way to the United States. They settled in the Boston, Massachusetts, area. Over the years, Sonia spoke thousands of times about the Holocaust to students and community organizations. She cofounded the Holocaust Center Boston North. In 2002, she and Elie Wiesel were appointed by President George W. Bush to the council advising the US Holocaust Memorial Museum in Washington.

Sonia published her Holocaust-era poems in her poignant memoir; *I Promised I Would Tell.* After her mother was taken from her, Sonia composed a poem called "In Memory of My Mother," which reads in part:

I still can hear

The words you spoke:

"You tell the world, my child."

I ***promised*** *I would*

Tell the world . . .

But where to find the words

To speak of

Innocence and love,

And tell how much it hurts . . .

About those faces

Weak and pale,

Those dizzy eyes around,

Six million lips

That whispered "help"

But never made a sound.

[My emphasis]

Sonia Schreiber Weitz died in 2010 at the age of 81, but not before she kept the promise to her mother that she would tell the world. A longtime friend, Harriet Wacks said: "In 1945, in the aftermath of the unthinkable, at the age of 16, Sonia chose life." Wacks added that Sonia "is a shining example of the survival of the human spirit."

Promises have contributed to our survival in the face of human conflict. Ancient villages that promised to settle disputes peacefully could flourish instead of perishing in battle. In our time, the member nations of NATO (North Atlantic Treaty Organization) have united to defend each other in the face of aggressors. NATO members operate on the mutually agreed-upon promise to view an armed attack against any one member to be an attack against them all.

I already cited one speech by NATO's Secretary General Jens Stoltenberg. Here's another example. In a well-received address to a Joint Meeting of the U.S. Congress (delivered on April 3, 2019), NATO Secretary General Jens Stoltenberg described NATO's mutual defense promise this way:

"Our Alliance was created by people who had lived through two devastating world wars. They knew only too well the horror, the suffering, and the human and material cost of war. They were determined that this should never happen again. And they were also determined to stand up to the expansion of the Soviet Union, which was taking control of its neighbors, crushing democracies, and oppressing their people.

"So, they founded NATO with a clear purpose: to preserve peace and to safeguard freedom. With an iron-clad commitment by all members of the Alliance to protect each other, *they made a solemn promise*: One for all and all for one. This commitment has served us well. Peace has been preserved; freedom maintained." [My emphasis.]

[Author's Note: Full disclosure… I worked as a speechwriter for top NATO leaders, including Secretary General Stoltenberg. However, I did not work on the two speeches cited in this book.]

A promise sends ripples outward, and these ripples encompass you, your family, your community, your state, your country and indeed the world. Think about it. If more people – hundreds of millions or more – make promises and begin to believe in their ability to reach more of their goals, build up their confidence about making positive change happen in their lives, and to achieve and receive more in terms of abundance and happiness, the cumulative effect will be a profound transformation in the world at large.

I think the world will be a much better place if millions of people embrace this unique power in their lives. Having "Make A Promise Day" recognized by thousands of jurisdictions around the world would be a major step forward.

I hope all readers of this book and all supporters of the power of making a promise will join this movement. Help me spread the word about the power of promises. Doing so will make a world of difference. Please consider making a promise – public or private – to do what you can to encourage adoption of this "Make A Promise Day" proclamation in as many jurisdictions as possible. And please let me know about any jurisdictions that issue the "Make A Promise Day" proclamation.

In addition to launching "Make A Promise Day," I'm taking this uplifting, personal empowerment message on the road by offering a keynote presentation – "The Power of Making a Promise." I'll be bringing this message to a wide variety of audiences, including schools and colleges, corporations, educational organizations, government agencies, and nonprofits.

I'm committed to getting this positive message about the power of making a promise out to millions of people around the world, through books like this one, through audio and videotapes, through keynotes and other presentations, through social media and media interviews. You name it. In fact, it's much more than a commitment, or a goal, or a resolution, or an intention. If you ask me: Ya Promise?" I will respond: "Yes! It's a promise!"

And I invite you to make your own promise to join me in this worldwide, heart-centered campaign. You – and the rest of the world – will be glad you did. I promise!

I want to end with a bonus promise story. To introduce it, I'll just mention that as I write these words on a rainy morning, I'm sipping coffee from one of my favorite mugs. The quote on the mug reportedly comes from John F. Kennedy, and it reads: "One person can make a difference, and everyone should try."

The spirit of making a difference sums up what harnessing your *PromisePower* is all about. And that spirit animates this final promise story. I hope you'll find it as inspiring as I do.

Barack Obama's Fired Up and Ready to Go!

When a young, little known, first-term Senator from Illinois was running for president in 2008, he made a promise that energized him and his long-shot campaign, giving him a heartwarming story to retell at various campaign events. You can watch Barack Obama tell this story on YouTube. And I highly recommend that you do.

Here's the gist of the story. In the early days of his unheralded campaign for the Democratic nomination, Obama traveled all over the country – north, south, east and west – trying to drum up support for his improbable candidacy. One day he found himself in South Carolina attending a conference of state legislators. He was hoping to meet political leaders who would be willing to endorse him. So, he was sitting next to a state legislator, and he asked for her endorsement. She said she liked him and that she would consider endorsing him if he promised to come to come to a meeting in Greenwood. Obama promised he would.

A six weeks later, after traveling around the country, Obama was back in South Carolina. He was dead tired after many long weeks on the road, and he was dragging himself to his hotel room after midnight hoping to get a good night sleep. One of his aides reminded him he had to get up at 6:30 in the morning because he ***promised*** to go to Greenwood.

Long story short, Obama reluctantly woke up the next morning after too little sleep and feeling terrible. He looked outside and it was pouring down rain. When he walked to his car his umbrella collapsed, leaving him soaking wet. The drive to Greenwood took an hour and a half. When he arrived in this tiny town he was feeling exhausted and not very hopeful that anything would come from this meeting. There were only about 20 people waiting to meet him and they didn't seem all that eager to be there either.

As he was introducing himself to everybody, he suddenly heard the state legislator he had met yell out from the back of the room: "Fired Up!" And everybody repeated, "Fired Up!" Then she yelled, "Ready to Go!" And everybody repeated, "Ready to Go!" And this chant was repeated several times. Obama joined in and soon he forgot his negative feelings and started to feel fired up. He was ready to go. Full of energy and no longer weighed down by negative thoughts or emotions. He soon learned that this state legislator was well known for starting meetings with this chant.

Obama sums up the lesson he took away: That a single voice can change a room and fill it with energy. And if a single voice could change a room, it could change a city. And if it could change a city it could change a state. And if it could change a state, it could change a country. And if it could change a country, it could change the world.

When Obama tells that story, the crowds respond with cheers and applause. They become energized and excited. The audiences become fired up and ready to go just like Obama was that rain-soaked morning in Greenwood, South Carolina.

He used that story to great effect during his successful campaigns for president in 2008 and again in 2012. And it all started with that ***promise*** he made to visit Greenwood. He had no idea that keeping his word to that state legislator would help him get elected president of the United.

As mentioned several times already, a promise made and kept creates a positive karmic halo effect. Unexpected, sometimes seemingly miraculous things tend to happen. This state legislator's voice changed that room. And then Barack Obama's voice, fired up and ready to go, changed the country and transformed the world.

That's the make-or-break power of a promise. It's the power we all possess that's captured in the four-part mantra, the four booster rockets featured so often in this book. I encourage you to read this mantra to yourself and out loud several times a day. And be sure to put your heart into it!

Make A Promise.

Keep Your Word.

Change Your Life.

Transform The World.

ACKNOWLEDGMENTS

This book would not exist in its current form without the unflagging patience and creative input of a special person – my partner and collaborator, Judy Lin. Judy has been instrumental in editing and shaping and reshaping the flow of the book's contents. While I take full responsibility for the book's shortcomings, I also recognize that the book has been improved dramatically by Judy's insightful suggestions. As I did with my previous book – *The Joy of Public Speaking* – I express my undying gratitude to Judy for her invaluable help throughout the challenging process of bringing this volume, at long last, into the world.

A host of friends and colleagues have contributed to the process of making this book a reality. I have already mentioned how indebted I am to Jack Canfield (www.JackCanfield.com) for his invaluable contributions. His remarkable foreword to the book speaks volumes. But his encouragement and support beyond the foreword also played an enormous role in boosting my confidence in the valuable role this book could play in the lives of others. I have told myself many times: "If Jack Canfield thinks this book contains a unique and powerful message, I must be on the right track." Jack's support steeled my spine and buoyed my spirits when times got tough. So, once again, I express my deep gratitude to Jack Canfield for his unwavering support.

A few others played pivotal roles at crucial moments. At an early stage in the book's journey from vague concept to publication, Norm Lapalme (www.ambassadorprogram.com) championed the book's message.

Steve Harrison (www.SteveHarrison.com) also played a key role in making this book possible. It was during Steve's "Quantum Leap Program" that I first met Jack Canfield. That meeting led to Jack's enthusiastic endorsement of my *PromisePower* project. So, I express my sincere gratitude to Steve for his role in helping to make possible the publication of *Harness Your PromisePower*.

I want to extend special thanks to the many people who contributed their personal promise stories that grace the book's pages. Their stories of promises made and kept are a true source of inspiration for me, and I hope through the publication of this book, for millions of others. These heartfelt stories have reminded me that there truly is something uniquely powerful about saying those two magic words: I Promise. These stories convince me that we truly can change our lives and transform the world, one person and one promise at a time.

Finally, a few words to countless friends who have heard me talk about the promise I made to my mother and the promise-related ideas in this book. Their willingness to listen and their expressions of enthusiasm for these ideas have made a huge difference in my determination to persevere in keeping my promise to publish this book. There were many times that I felt this was a hopeless pipedream instead of a powerful promise. Because so many friends have voiced their faith in the power of making a promise, my confidence in the book's significance has been reinforced time and again over the years. My sincere thanks to all of you.

RESOURCES/CONNECTIONS

My Speaker/Author Website: www.MatthewCossolotto.com

Send Me Your Personal Promise Stories:
MatthewPromisePower@gmail.com

(Including any inspiring promise stories you come across in the media, or in books, movies, etc.)

Contact Me for Updates: MatthewPromisePower@gmail.com

(Send me an email to submit comments or ideas and to sign up for periodic updates about my books, speaking engagements, merchandise, launching a "What's Your Promise?" podcast, etc. I would love to hear from you!)

Various Personal Empowerment Gift Items Under Consideration

- *PromisePower* Bands
- *PromisePower* Rubber Bands
- Ya Promise? T-Shirts, Coffee Mugs, etc.
- Make a Promise Day Greeting Cards, Coffee Mugs, etc.
- What's Your Promise?: T-Shirts, Coffee Mugs, etc.
- Seven Tips for Making and Keeping Promises: Posters, Coffee Mugs, etc.
- No Failure Zone: Posters, T-Shirts, Coffee Mugs, etc.
- The Six Axioms of Personal Empowerment: Posters, etc.

[Note: Some gift items are already available via www.Zazzle.com/thecoz, but other sites may be used in the future. Newsletter updates will keep you posted on developments.]

Websites for Selected Friends/Experts/Luminaries/ Organizations Whose Promise Stories Are Included in This Book

Andrea Adams-Miller (https://igniteyourrelationship.com/)

John Assaraf (www.JohnAssaraf.com)

Kody Bateman (https://www.sendoutcards.com)

President Joe Biden (https://joebiden.com/)

Oral Lee Brown (https://www.oralleebrownfoundation.org)

Brendon Burchard (www.BrendonBurchard.com)

Chris Cade (www.ChrisCade.com)

Jack Canfield (www.JackCanfield.com)

Diane DiResta (www.DiResta.com)

Roger Federer (www.RogerFederer.com)

Roslyn Franken (www.RoslynFranken.com)

Victor Garcia (https://www.eightfigureempires.com)

Gail Lynne Goodwin (www.InspireMeToday.com)

LeBron James (www.LeBronJames.com)

Stefania Lucchetti (https://stefanialucchetti.it/en/)

Princess Merrilee (https://merrileeofsolana.com)

Martina Navratilova (https://www.martinanavratilova.com)

Todd Newton (https://www.toddnewtononline.com/)

Marques Ogden (https://www.marquesogden.com)

Grace Redman (https://www.daretoachieve.com/)

Jin Kyu Robertson (https://housemaidtoharvard.blogspot.com/2012/02/from-housemaid-to-harvard-phd-jin.html)

Sonia Schreiber Weitz (https://www.amazon.com/Promised-Would-Tell-Testimony-Holocaust/dp/0961584130)

Pam Shriver (https://www.pamelashriver.com)

Tara Taylor (https://tarataylor.ca/)

Laura Templeton (https://30secondsuccess.com)

The Optimist Creed, Optimist International [https://www.optimist.org/member/creed.cfm.]

Brian Tracy (www.briantracy.com)

St. Jude Children's Research Hospital [https://www.stjude.org]

(Danny and Marlo Thomas)

Oprah Winfrey (www.Oprah.com)

A FEW FRIENDS/COLLEAGUES WHO ENCOURAGED ME ALONG THE WAY

Rick Frishman (www.RickFrishman.com)

Steve Harrison (www.SteveHarrison.com)

Norm Lapalme (www.ambassadorprogram.com)

Peggy McColl (www.peggymccoll.com)

Brian Proctor, Publisher (www.InsightoftheDay.com)

APPENDIX A

The Six Axioms of Personal Empowerment

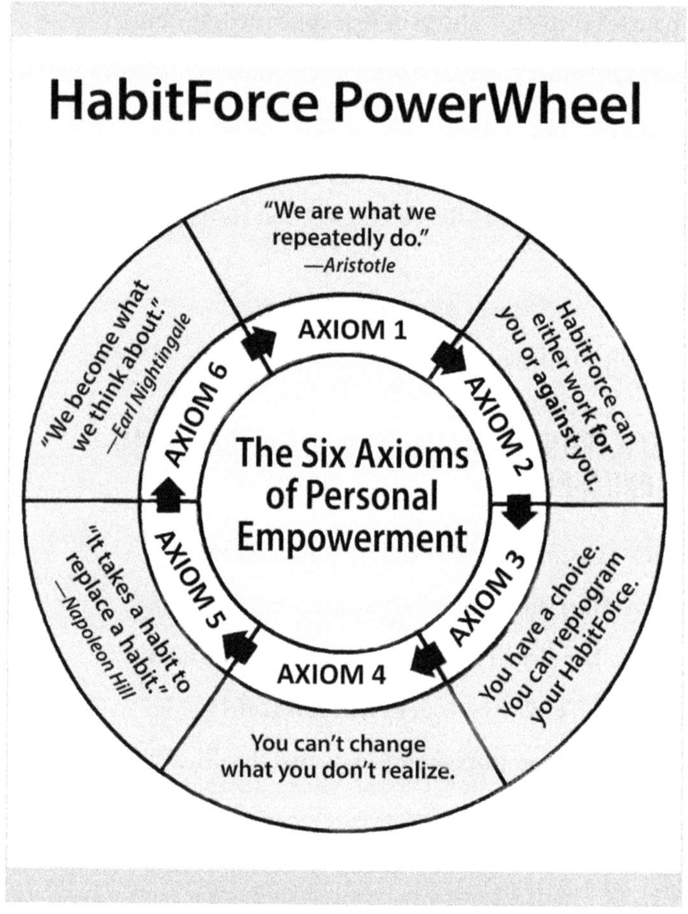

APPENDIX B

7 Tips for Making and Keeping Promises

7 TIPS FOR MAKING AND KEEPING PROMISES

By Matthew Cossolotto
Author of *Harness Your PromisePower*
Matthew@MatthewCossolotto.com / www.MatthewCossolotto.com

1. START SMALL! Get started by identifying and promising to reach a few of relatively small, quickly accomplished goals. Ease your way into this. Slowly build your promise-keeping, achievement muscles. Establish the habit of keeping your promises.

2. BE SPECIFIC! Use the G.P.S. Success Formula: From Goals to Promises = Success. Turn concrete goals into heartfelt promises. Don't be vague, unclear or wishy washy about your promises. Keep in mind that you can *change* a goal, but you can only *break* a promise. Most people are loath to break their promises.

3. BE SELECTIVE! Continue to use the G.P.S. Success Formula. Pick one or two goals and turn them into promises. If you go overboard with too many promises, you'll lose track and get distracted and frustrated. So be selective. A promise is like a goal on steroids.

4. WRITE IT! Don't just say the words. Write them down. A written promise, signed into law by your own hand, can be more binding and powerful than a verbal promise.

5. SHARE IT! Share your promise with others. Make it public. Hold a "promise making" ceremony on "Make a Promise Day" (May 4th) or some other special occasion like Mother's Day or Father's Day. Make a promise instead of a wish on your birthday. Post your promises on social media.

6. COMMIT EMOTIONALLY! Make a promise to someone you care about. Look that person in the eye and say the two magic words: "I Promise." A promise comes from the heart. Know in your heart that failure is not an option.

7. FOLLOW THROUGH! Remember, when you make a promise your integrity is on the line. You must follow through. Make a solemn promise to yourself, to a higher power, or to someone you care about -- or all three at once! And keep your word! Keeping promises creates a kind of positive karmic halo effect. Bask in the positive karma of making and keeping a promise.

APPENDIX C

Top 10 Promises for a SUCCESSFUL Life

[Author's Note: These "Top 10 Promises" appear in the book as promises 20-29 in my "A Promise a Day – 30 Days to a Promising Future" program.

The Top 10 Promises for a SUCCESSFUL Life

DAY 20, PROMISE #20 –
S. "I PROMISE... TO SHOULDER RESPONSIBILITY FOR MY LIFE AND DESTINY, PLACING MYSELF BEHIND THE WHEEL, IN CHARGE WITH NO EXCUSES."

DAY 21, PROMISE #21 –
U. "I PROMISE... TO UNITE WITH EAGLES BY ASSOCIATING WITH POSITIVE ROLE MODELS OF PERSONAL ACHIEVEMENT, INTEGRITY AND SER VICE."

DAY 22, PROMISE #22 –
C. "I PROMISE... TO CARPE DIEM – SEIZE THE DAY – REGULARLY TAKING ACTION AND SEIZING OPPORTUNITIES TO ACHIEVE MY GOALS, DREAMS, PURPOSE ... AND KEEP MY PROMISES."

DAY 23, PROMISE #23 –
C. "I PROMISE... TO CULTIVATE ENTHUSIASM, PURPOSE AND HAPPINESS IN MY LIFE BY DISCOVERING, EMBRACING AND PURSUING MY TRUE PASSIONS. THIS IS NOT A DRESS REHEARSAL!"

DAY 24, PROMISE #24 –
E. "I PROMISE... TO EMPOWER MYSELF BY HARNESSING MY HABITFORCE AND BY CONTINUOUS SELF-IMPROVEMENT TO REACH MY PEAK POTENTIAL IN LIFE."

DAY 25, PROMISE #25 –
S. "I PROMISE... TO SET MY COURSE IN ALIGNMENT WITH MY DHARMA, MY PURPOSE, MY PASSION, AND TOWARD MY DREAMS, GOALS AND PROMISES."

DAY 26, PROMISE #26 –
S. "I PROMISE... TO SOW OPTIMISM AND JOY IN MY LIFE AND THE LIVES OF OTHERS, RECOGNIZING THAT HAPPINESS IS THE ULTIMATE SUCCESS."

DAY 27, PROMISE #27 –
F. "I PROMISE... TO FOCUS ON FINANCIAL FREEDOM, PURPOSEFULLY CREATING AND RECEIVING ABUNDANCE FOR MYSELF AND GENEROUSLY HELPING OTHERS DO THE SAME."

DAY 28, PROMISE #28 –
U. "I PROMISE... TO UNLEASH THE POWER OF GRATITUDE BY COUNTING MY BLESSINGS AND APPRECIATING DAILY THE MANY THINGS I'M GRATEFUL FOR."

DAY 29, PROMISE #29 –
L. "I PROMISE... TO LOVE... TO LOVE MY LIFE, TO GENUINELY FEEL AND EXPRESS LOVE, AND TO CONSCIOUSLY CREATE A LASTING LEGACY OF LOVE."

APPENDIX D

Model "Make a Promise Day" Proclamation

[Join the *PromisePower* movement. Please urge local, state, national, and international authorities and various organization to adopt this Proclamation.]

Office of ____________________

____

(Insert Town, City, County, State/Province, Country or Organization)

Make a PROMISE Day

May 4th

May The Fourth Be With You!

Contact: Matthew Cossolotto, www.MakeAPromiseDay.com

PROCLAMATION

WHEREAS: MAKE A PROMISE DAY IS THE ONLY UNOFFICIAL "HOLIDAY" DEDICATED TO PERSONAL EMPOWERMENT, GOAL ACHIEVEMENT AND INTEGRITY ENHANCEMENT, AND;

WHEREAS: MAKE A PROMISE DAY ENCOURAGES INDIVIDUALS TO TURN IMPORTANT GOALS INTO HEARTFELT PROMISES, THEREBY INCREASING THE PROBABILITY OF REACHING THOSE GOALS, AND;

WHEREAS: CELEBRATING MAKE A PROMISE DAY WILL HAVE THE EFFECT OF ENHANCING ACCOUNTABILITY, PERSONAL RESPONSIBILITY AND INTEGRITY, AND;

THE (INSERT TITLE ____________________) RECOGNIZES THE VALUE OF HIGHLIGHTING THE POWER OF MAKING AND KEEPING PROMISES ON THE PART OF LOCAL STUDENTS, TEACHERS, COMMUNITY ORGANIZATIONS, BUSINESSES AND POLITICAL LEADERS;

NOW, THEREFORE, I, (NAME AND TITLE ____________________), DO HEREBY PROCLAIM MAY 4, (INSERT YEAR ____) AND EACH YEAR THEREAFTER TO BE MAKE A PROMISE DAY AND ENCOURAGE ORGANIZATIONS AND INDIVIDUAL MEMBERS OF THE COMMUNITY TO CELEBRATE THIS VERY IMPORTANT DAY IN A MANNER THEY DEEM TO BE SUITABLE AND APPROPRIATE.

(SIGNED ____________________) (DATE ____________________)

ABOUT THE AUTHOR

Matthew Cossolotto is an author, guest speaker, executive speechwriter, and speech coach. He works with leaders and aspiring leaders who want to advance their careers and enhance their leadership success by reaching their peak potential, on and off the podium. He also provides speechwriting, speech coaching, and PodiumPower! and The Joy of Public Speaking workshops and forums designed to help corporations and other organizations enhance the public speaking and leadership skills of their executives.

His high-level leadership communications career spans the corridors of power and influence on both sides of the Atlantic. He has served as a speechwriter for top officials at NATO headquarters in Brussels, Belgium, and for the Speaker of the U.S. House of Representatives.

Matthew's eight years on Capitol Hill included serving as legislative assistant for Representative Leon Panetta. He has coached or penned speeches for a wide range of corporate and academic leaders – from the Chancellor of UCLA to CEOs and other senior executives at GTE (now Verizon), Pepsi-Cola, MCI, MasterCard, LaFarge, Neustar, and many more.

In 1992, Matthew helped found the Center for Voting and Democracy (now Fair Vote www.fairvote.org) and served as president and board chair for five years. Matthew is also the author of *The Almanac of European Politics* and *The Almanac of Transatlantic Politics.*

The Joy of Public Speaking – published in 2021 – is the first book in Matthew's personal empowerment trilogy. *Harness Your PromisePower* is the second book in the trilogy. The third book – *Harness Your HabitForce* – is due for publication in the coming months. These books and related coaching and speaking programs feature a unique combination of three interconnected "power tools" – Speaking, Habits, and Promises – that fuel Matthew's Triad Empowerment System.

As a guest speaker, workshop leader, and speech coach, Matthew has shared his ideas and expertise with a wide range of domestic and international audiences, including corporations, associations, government agencies, conferences, schools, community groups, and nonprofits/NGOs. For more information about Matthew's coaching programs, leadership communication services, and Personal Empowerment Programs (PEPTalks), visit www.MatthewCossolotto.com.

Finally, here's one more public promise: Matthew promises to create and deliver a series of TED or TEDx talks based on the ideas featured in his Triad Empowerment System: Speaking, Habits, Promises.

www.ingramcontent.com/pod-product-compliance
Ingram Content Group UK Ltd.
Pitfield, Milton Keynes, MK11 3LW, UK
UKHW020417250726
13967UKWH00007B/2692